TROUBLE SHOOTING GASOLINE MARINE ENGINES

JOHN FLEMING

Editor: Jerry Renninger

Bristol Fashion Publications, Inc.
Harrisburg, Pennsylvania

Troubleshooting Gasoline Marine Engines - John Fleming

Published by Bristol Fashion Publications, Inc.

Copyright © 2001 by John Fleming. All rights reserved.

No part of this book may be reproduced or used in any form or by any means-graphic, electronic, mechanical, including photocopying, recording, taping or information storage and retrieval systems-without written permission of the publisher.

BRISTOL FASHION PUBLICATIONS AND THE AUTHOR HAVE MADE EVERY EFFORT TO INSURE THE ACCURACY OF THE INFORMATION PROVIDED IN THIS BOOK BUT ASSUMES NO LIABILITY WHATSOEVER FOR SAID INFORMATION OR THE CONSEQUENCES OF USING THE INFORMATION PROVIDED IN THIS BOOK.

ISBN: 1-892216-28-0
LCCN: 00-136117

Contribution acknowledgments

Inside Graphics: By the author or as noted
Cover Design: John P. Kaufman
Cover Photo: Mercury Marine

Troubleshooting Gasoline Marine Engines - John Fleming

Troubleshooting Gasoline Marine Engines - John Fleming

DEDICATION

In my own humble way I have attempted to approach each engine I have encountered as a challenge -- a mystery whose secrets I sought to unfold, one by one. I once thought the greatest mysteries to be found were represented by those marvelous pieces of metal.

As the years passed, I watched my children born and saw them grow into fine adults. Next came grandchildren, and they, too, have embarked upon the journey. Slowly I began to realize a new reality: Apart from whatever immediate mystery they seek to solve, they must find some way to solve the mystery of life. Perhaps they will become truly able diagnosticians. I dearly hope so.

That said, I dedicate this volume to my grandchildren: Fred Dinkler IV, Allison G. Dinkler and Alexander M. Freas.

Troubleshooting Gasoline Marine Engines - John Fleming

Troubleshooting Gasoline Marine Engines - John Fleming

INTRODUCTION

Diagnostics is the most difficult job for the medical doctor. It is also the most difficult job facing the engine tech. Virtually any doctor can treat the patient if he/she can diagnose the problem. Not every doctor can do this. Neither can every engine technician.

Today, many engine systems are electronic in nature, and diagnosis is largely done by laptop computer. Yet, many are not electronically controlled. Starters, alternators, manifolds and even the entire engine assembly are still mechanical in nature.

Problems that attack these systems and assemblies are still approached in the same manner as they have been for decades. Many engines have no electronic controls at all. I doubt there will ever come a time when basic skills are not required of the marine mechanic.

If mechanics are to be complete in knowledge and understanding of their chosen career, they must be able practitioners of the diagnostic science. There is no instrument on earth that can replace human intelligence.

What are the elements of a good diagnostician? First and foremost, you must understand why the engine works. Service manuals are available to describe in detail the separate operations required to repair or service any given part of the engine. These are the skills that a majority of mechanics possess.

The challenge is to decide which of these common skills are needed to restore the ailing engine to proper

Troubleshooting Gasoline Marine Engines - John Fleming

condition. Happily, the well-trained mechanic has many skills ready to employ, yet must decide which of these skills to use. In making this decision, you will use the senses of sight and sound, smell and feel. When you have a complete grasp of the engine and its many moods, you will literally be able to hear it talk and feel its pains.

One who knows how to perform these functions will always have a job. However, the mechanic who knows which of them to use at a given time will always be the boss!

This book will not tell you to set the ignition points at .020", nor to open the air screw on the carburetor 1-1/2 turns. It will advise how to decide if the points should be opened or closed, and whether you should turn the air screw or leave it alone.

I have proposed many problems and offered my own solutions. The mechanic, amateur or professional, may have alternatives. If they work for you, and you are more comfortable in their use, employ them. If you have no solutions or simply wish to add options to your arsenal, I hope my offerings prove helpful.

John Fleming

Troubleshooting Gasoline Marine Engines - John Fleming

TABLE OF CONTENTS

INTRODUCTION

CHAPTER ONE   Page 15
     THE THEORY OF TROUBLESHOOTING

CHAPTER TWO   Page 19
     INITIAL APPROACH

CHAPTER THREE   Page 25
     SECOND APPROACH

CHAPTER FOUR   Page 35
     TEST THE FUEL SYSTEM

CHAPTER FIVE   Page 41
     THE TUNE-UP

CHAPTER SIX   Page 49
     LOW COMPRESSION - HOW TO PROCEED

CHAPTER SEVEN   Page 55
     VISUAL SIGNS

CHAPTER EIGHT   Page 61
     AUDIBLE SIGNALS

Troubleshooting Gasoline Marine Engines - John Fleming

CHAPTER NINE — Page 69
    THE WIRING HARNESS

CHAPTER TEN — Page 77
    ACCESSORIES

CHAPTER ELEVEN — Page 83
    WATER-RELATED ACCESSORIES

CHAPTER TWELVE — Page 93
    DISASSEMBLY AND INSPECTION OF THE CYLINDER HEADS

CHAPTER THIRTEEN — Page 101
    BEFORE YOU DISASSEMBLE THE ENGINE

CHAPTER FOURTEEN — Page 107
    COMPLETE ENGINE DISASSEMBLY

CHAPTER FIFTEEN — Page 113
    PREPARING THE ENGINE FOR MACHINE WORK

CHAPTER SIXTEEN — Page 119
    REASSEMBLE THE ENGINE

CHAPTER SEVENTEEN — Page 127
    COMPLETE THE ASSEMBLY

CHAPTER EIGHTEEN — Page 131
    FINAL ENGINE ASSEMBLY

CHAPTER NINETEEN — Page 139
    START-UP PROCEDURE

CHAPTER TWENTY — Page 141
    PROBLEMS & CAUSE

Troubleshooting Gasoline Marine Engines - John Fleming

CHAPTER TWENTY-ONE   Page 149
    TROUBLESHOOT THE ACCESSORIES

CHAPTER TWENTY-TWO   Page 155
    FINAL WORDS

Troubleshooting Gasoline Marine Engines - John Fleming

CHAPTER ONE
THE THEORY OF TROUBLESHOOTING

Begin with the principle requirements for engine operation. Establish in your mind the things that the engine needs to function properly, and never forget them. When the engine does not run, it will always be because one of the following is missing.

Every engine must have six elementary things available in order to run properly:

1. A combustible fuel
2. Air
3. Air in the proper proportions with fuel
4. Balanced compression
5. A proper source of ignition
6. All of the above provided at the correct time

Every problem that the troubleshooter encounters will result from the loss or failure of one or more of these elements. Diagnosis must begin with these concepts in mind, but there must be no diagnosis until you have all of the facts. Look over the engine carefully. Gather all the information you can, and do so as rapidly as possible. Usually, the engine operator is the best source of primary information, but anyone commonly aboard the vessel when it is operating may also be a good source.

Troubleshooting Gasoline Marine Engines - John Fleming

Begin with an open mind, yet try to categorize the problem and isolate it into one or more of the areas listed above. By doing this you narrow your search to a smaller number of parts or pieces. You also save a great deal of expensive time that might be wasted by looking in the wrong place.

Perhaps this sounds a bit too simple, but it is not. It is a very logical procedure. Think about the things that have gone wrong with your engines over the years. No matter what eventually proved to be wrong, every problem revolved around one or more of those six categories listed above. As this book continues, we will detail each of the systems that help the engine to function, such as carburetors, injectors, ignition systems etc. We will tie each into the total operation of the engine and describe the symptoms of failure. We will also demonstrate into which categories the problem fits and show why. In the future you should be able to look at any engine, make a few checks, and at least know the area in which the problem lies. I can not over-emphasize the importance of this elimination process.

With his time billed at a record-high sum, the mechanic must be able to show results for each hour. By placing the problem in a specific category and understanding which of the engine's parts are utilized within that category, the diagnostician knows immediately which part or group of parts is suspect.

For example. if your engine suddenly stops, first make two checks. Look for fuel at the carburetor and spark at the plugs. We will begin with fuel and move on to spark.

Possible sources for fuel problems are:

1. The fuel pump
2. Fuel lines
3. Fuel filter
4. Fuel tank pickup
5. Fuel supply

Troubleshooting Gasoline Marine Engines - John Fleming

Among the parts listed above is the likely source of your problem. You now have a quick list of the potential sources of your trouble and you have narrowed your search to an easily managed area.

Assume that there is no spark. The parts involved in the production of a spark are:

1. Battery
2. Battery switch
3. Wiring harness
4. Ignition switch
5. Coil
6. Distributor
7. Plug wires
8. The plugs themselves

The part or parts needed to restore a proper spark lies somewhere within this group. You do not know exactly which is to blame, but you know where to look.

Always begin with the assumption that the factory engineers have spent many hours perfecting this engine. In the early going, follow their lead. Yet, no engineer or designer can make allowances for every special circumstance.

Ask if you need closer maintenance intervals than the factory recommends. Is the oil doing well, or should I change the viscosity? Are my spark plugs too hot/cold? Are the jets too rich/lean in the carburetor? Is the factory-spec ignition timing too high?

Some of the descriptions and operations in this book will be redundant, that is, recognizable in more than a single chapter. This is because a number of problems can be approached, recognized or repaired in more than a single way.

You may benefit from reading *The Complete Guide To Gasoline Marine Engines* (also available from Bristol Fashion Publications) before beginning this one. It gives proper names to each of the parts and features of the gasoline engine and describes their function. It covers the theory of operating

Troubleshooting Gasoline Marine Engines - John Fleming

gasoline engines very thoroughly. The benefits of using the two books together may prove remarkable.

Troubleshooting Gasoline Marine Engines - John Fleming

CHAPTER TWO
INITIAL APPROACH

Begin with the most basic assumption: the engine does not start. There are two possibilities. In the first, the engine will not react to operation of the ignition switch. Accordingly, we must start from genesis. In the second, the starter circuit will show at least some signs of life; some systems will function.

As described in Chapter One, think of the starting system. Its parts are:

1. A storage battery
2. A battery switch that delivers current to all systems, including the starting circuit (main breaker)
3. A conductor to deliver current from the battery to the ignition switch (light-gauge wire)
4. A separate conductor to deliver current from the ignition switch to the input side of the starter solenoid (light-gauge wire)
5. The starter solenoid itself
6. A conductor to deliver current from the storage battery to the starter solenoid (heavy-gauge wire)
7. A conductor to deliver current from the solenoid to the starter motor (heavy-gauge wire)

Let us now consider how the starter system works. Begin with the battery main breaker in the On position; 12-volt current should be available at the ignition switch. Turn the ignition switch to the Start position; this should furnish 12-volt

Troubleshooting Gasoline Marine Engines - John Fleming

current to the low-amperage (or switching) side of the starter solenoid.

The starter solenoid is, in fact, a switch unto itself. It operates on an electromagnet that engages as current is fed to it and disengages when the current is no longer present. The starter solenoid should engage and deliver high-amperage starting current to the starter motor. The bendix gear should engage the flywheel, and the engine should begin to turn. This system works regardless of whether the engine has electronic or conventional ignition, carburetion or injection.

Check all the vital liquids in the engine before making any attempt to start it. Never mind that someone may have tried to do so before you got there. Inspect the oil and water levels, open the hatches, sniff for fumes, then operate the blower if possible. Now return to Paragraph One and our two possibilities.

1. You have turned the ignition switch to Start and absolutely nothing happened. What does this indicate? The problem lies in one of those seven parts listed previously, and it is probably at the ignition switch or somewhere between it and the battery.

Why not farther down the line? Remember the premise: you turned the switch to Start and nothing happened. There are gauges, warning lights and other systems that are energized when the ignition switch is turned on. The solenoid may fail or the starter may not engage, but it is highly unlikely that all systems will fail at one time. It is a pretty safe bet that the ignition switch is not delivering current to the systems downstream, and thus you have already cut the problem in half.

Now you need a volt/ohmmeter (VOM) to measure current and resistance as required. Turn the VOM to the Voltage setting and adjust it within the 25-volt range.

With the ignition switch in the Start position, press the red lead to the output side of the switch and the black lead to any ground. It should read 12 volts, but it almost surely will not do so. Next, moving in succession, test the input side of the ignition switch. Is 12-volt current available there?

Troubleshooting Gasoline Marine Engines - John Fleming

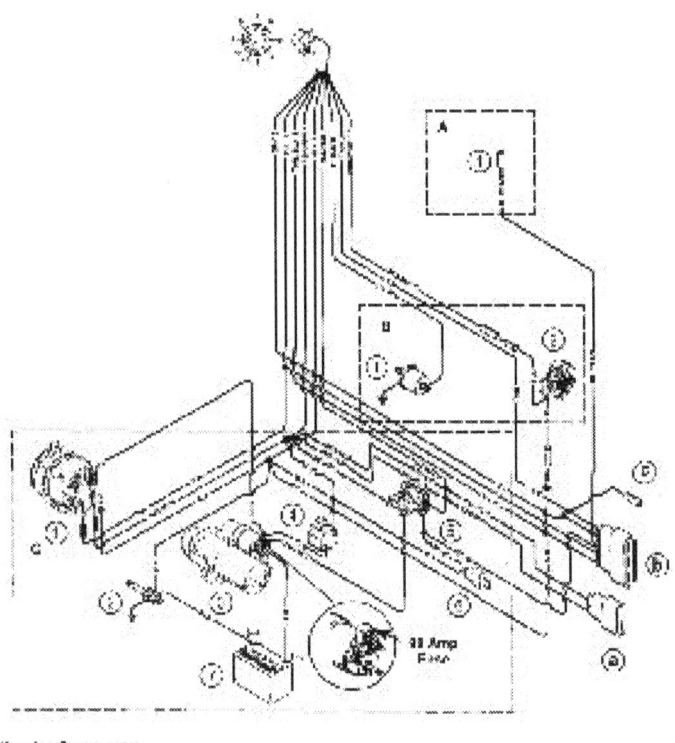

A - Audio Warning Components
   1 - Oil Pressure Switch
B - Instrumentation Components
   1 - Oil Pressure Sender
   2 - Trim Sender
C - Charging and Starting Components
   1 - Alternator
   2 - Starter Stud
   3 - Starter
   4 - Circuit Breaker
   5 - Starter Slave Solenoid
   6 - Jumper Wire Connection
   7 - Battery
   a - Positive Power Wire To EFI System Harness
   b - Harness Connector To EFI System Harness
   c - Accessory Tachometer Lead

Figure 1
Courtesy of Mercury Marine

Starting and charging system.

If 12-volt current is available to the ignition switch but not through it, replace the switch. Otherwise, move backwards

Troubleshooting Gasoline Marine Engines - John Fleming

towards the battery. In succession, check the wires leading to the ignition switch and their terminals. Examine the main battery switch and finally the battery itself. If the battery is dead, remove it from the boat. Do not waste time with this. Always check the level of the electrolyte, place the battery on a charger, bring it up to full charge and run a load test. If the battery satisfies in all respects, you can return it to the boat. Otherwise, replace it. There is some reason why the battery failed. Be certain that the present or replacement battery you're about to install has sufficient capacity, then check the systems. Turn off all switches in the circuit, attach the black (ground) wire to the battery. Set the VOM on Voltage and insert the leads of the VOM between the battery's red lead (positive) lead and black (positive) lead.

If you get a reading, there is a continuous load on the battery from somewhere, even if the switches are off. This is probably why the battery was discharged, and you must find the source of this drainage. If the VOM shows no reading, you're ready to attach the red (hot) lead to the battery.

2. Assume you have turned the ignition switch to Start and get movement from the gauges, yet nothing else happens.

Look at the voltmeter on the instrument panel. Does it read 11.5 volts or higher? If not, you can go back to the battery. You have current to and through the ignition switch, but it is not sufficient to operate the starting systems. If the reading is between 11.5 volts and 12.2 volts, you can move on to the starter solenoid. Check all conductors and terminals along the way.

With the ignition switch in the Start position, check the input side of the solenoid for current. None? You have a faulty conductor somewhere. If there is ample current at the solenoid, you should hear a healthy click when the switch is turned to Start. If this sound is absent, the solenoid is faulty.

If the anticipated click occurs, the solenoid switch is operating properly, and you now have to consider the heavy-duty starting circuit. With the starter switch closed and the starter solenoid energized, check for proper current in the

Troubleshooting Gasoline Marine Engines - John Fleming

heavy cables at the input side of the solenoid.

If there is not sufficient current (10.5 to 12.2 volts) at the input side, trace the heavy-gauge wiring and all terminals back to the battery. If there is proper current available but the nice, crisp click brings no result, check the output side of the solenoid. If there is not sufficient current available there, the solenoid switch is not operating properly. Replace it.

Assume you have a good solenoid, a nice loud click and current through the solenoid. The starter motor turns but the engine does not turn over (that is not the worst kind of news). You have a bendix that does not engage. Remove the starter, repair and replace.

What if the starter engages fully into the flywheel with plenty of starting torque but the engine fails to turn over? This may be bad news indeed. So long as the starting circuit's in good shape and the battery is hot, your problem lies with a locked or partially locked engine.

There should be other indicators. When a good starting system is fully engaged, a great deal of energy is released and considerable heat generated. Starter motors do not ordinarily turn for extended periods of time. Fifteen seconds on the starter motor should be sufficient for a properly tuned engine. Thus, the heat generated during the starting process is generally manageable, but if the engine does not turn over, the heat builds rapidly. Battery leads become overheated and begin to smoke.

Never hold the ignition switch in the Start position when the engine is locked up. All sorts of unhappy things will occur, including the destruction of various parts of the starting circuit. Given that all parts of the starting circuit are working properly and the engine refuses to rotate, you can cease work on the starting system and look elsewhere.

A few items are worth examining here. The storage battery is considered to be effectively discharged when the available voltage is reduced to 10.5 volts. Many mechanics look for any voltage at all and believe that if the battery produces 12-volt current when fully charged, six volts is a half-

Troubleshooting Gasoline Marine Engines - John Fleming

charge. Nothing could be further from the truth. In fact, if the battery has the proper capacity, it should hold 10.5 volts or more during the starting cycle. With the starter engaged and the engine turning over, the reading on your voltmeter should remain at least that high. If it does not, you're overloading the battery.

Watch the voltmeter on your instrument panel. Assuming that the battery normally has the proper capacity, a severe drop in voltage during start-up can be an early sign of imminent battery failure or possibly other problems in the system. They are:

1. A dragging starter
2. A partially locked engine

Remember the parts of the starting system, the function of each and the sequence in which they operate. When you have these things firmly set in your mind, the job of troubleshooting is simple. What if the starting system operates properly, the engine rotates at a satisfactory speed but it does not start? Read on.

CHAPTER THREE
SECOND APPROACH

Let us suppose that the engine has a proper starting system and that it turns over in response to the ignition switch. In fact, it does so in a spirited and satisfying manner, but nonetheless it fails to start.

If this is an engine with an electronic fuel injector (EFI) high-energy ignition system (HEI) and an electronic control unit (ECU) or computer to coordinate both systems, we can resort to the laptop. Plug it into the proper ports and proceed according to the instruction manual.

If it is a carbureted engine, it employs either a conventional ignition system with points and a condenser or a capacitive discharge (CD) system. In this situation we will begin with the ignition and thoroughly test its function. This is logical because, should we fail to find our problem here, we will next address the fuel system, and this may result in some small fuel spillage. Because we do not wish to light up the engine room with a stray spark, we now address the ignition system:

1. Storage battery
2. Wiring harness with conductors
3. Ignition switch
4. Conductor to coil
5. Resistor
5. Starter solenoid
6. Ignition coil

Troubleshooting Gasoline Marine Engines - John Fleming

7. Conductor from coil to distributor (low voltage)
8. Coil lead (high voltage)
9. Distributor
10. High-tension spark plug leads
11. Spark plugs

I'll begin this discussion with the methods of troubleshooting that are useful for all types of ignition systems. Then we will move on to methods specific to:

1. Conventional points-actuated distributors
2. Simple capacitive-discharge electronic distributors

In the parts list you no doubt recognize the starter solenoid as an unusual inclusion. I'll explain this fully as the chapter progresses.

HOW DOES IT WORK?
CONVENTIONAL SYSTEMS WITH POINTS

The storage battery furnishes current to the starter switch, and the starter switch delivers current to the low-voltage side of the ignition coil. The ignition coil should pass this current across the windings to the distributor and finally to the ignition points. The high-tension side of the coil should produce a blue/white spark and deliver it to the distributor rotor. The distributor rotor should deliver spark to the appropriate cylinder only. The spark plug leads should deliver the high-voltage spark to the plug, and the spark plug should discharge inside the cylinder. If any of these things do not happen in sequence, the engine will not start.

Troubleshooting Gasoline Marine Engines - John Fleming

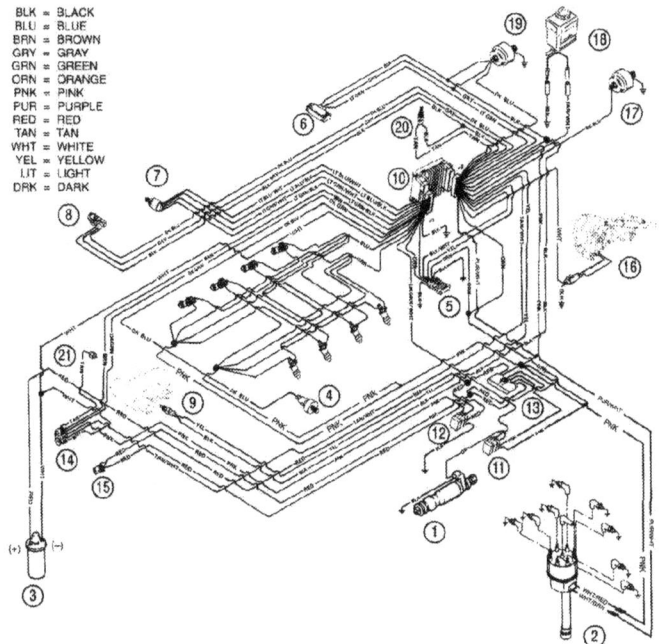

BLK = BLACK
BLU = BLUE
BRN = BROWN
GRY = GRAY
GRN = GREEN
ORN = ORANGE
PNK = PINK
PUR = PURPLE
RED = RED
TAN = TAN
WHT = WHITE
YEL = YELLOW
LIT = LIGHT
DRK = DARK

NOTE: All BLACK wires with a ground symbol are interconnected within the EFI system harness.

NOTE: Component position and orientation shown is arranged for visual clarity and ease of circuit identification.

1 - Fuel Pump
2 - Distributor
3 - Coil
4 - Knock Sensor (KS) Module
5 - Data Link Connector (DLC)
6 - Manifold Absolute Pressure (MAP) Sensor
7 - Idle Air Control (IAC)
8 - Throttle Position (TP) Sensor
9 - Engine Coolant Temperature (ECT) Sensor
10- Electronic Control Module (ECM)
11- Fuel Pump Relay
12- Ignition/System Relay
13- Fuse (15 Amp) Fuel Pump, Fuse (15 Amp) ECM/DLC/Battery,Fuse (10 Amp) ECM/Injector/Ignition/Knock Module
14- Harness Connector To Starting/Charging Harness
15- Positive (+) Power Wire To Engine Circuit Breaker
16- Shift Plate (Not used on Bravo models)
17- Oil Pressure (Audio Warning System)
18- Gear Lube Bottle
19- Fuel Pressure Switch
20- Water Temperature Sender

Figure 2
Courtesy of Mercury Marine

Fuel and ignition system.

HOW TO CORRECT THE PROBLEM

For any marine gasoline engine, I begin tracing spark problems at the end of the system and work backwards. First remove the lead from the spark plug on #1 cylinder, then remove the plug.

We now want to test for spark. I have saved several old plugs and broken off the ground strap at the side of the plug. The remaining tip has about a 3/8" gap between the side of the plug and the electrode (this makes a great test plug). There are relatively inexpensive tools you can buy, but this plug works fine, and it is free.

Install the test plug into the boot on the plug wire and ground the base on any metal part of the engine. Forget the paint. The spark will penetrate paint quite easily if it is very strong. Now turn the engine over with the starter. You should get a strong, blue/white spark and hear a slightly audible snap. If you get this reaction on a rapid and uninterrupted basis as the engine revolves, the trouble is probably in your spark plugs.

NO SPARK

Try a few more leads. If some spark but others do not, you probably have faulty plug wires. It is seldom that all of them fail at once. Still no spark? It is time to move back to the distributor.

THE HIGH-TENSION SIDE OF THE DISTRIBUTOR

The distributor has two systems, one high-voltage and one low-voltage. The parts of the high-tension system are the rotor and the distributor cap.

Remove the high-tension coil wire at the distributor end. With a pair of insulated pliers to hold the high-tension coil lead, space it about 1/2" from the cylinder head and turn the engine over with the starter. You should get a spark as described above. If you do, the problem is somewhere inside the distributor. Why? The coil is making adequate fire and delivering it to the distributor. In short, fire is going in but

Troubleshooting Gasoline Marine Engines - John Fleming

nothing is coming out. Open the distributor, then check the rotor and distributor cap. Look for cracks in the cap or rotor and carbon tracks or moisture in the distributor cap. Your problem should be in one or both. What if no fire appears? Install a new coil wire and repeat the test. If you get an adequate spark, the problem is the high- tension coil lead, and you're successful. If there is still not a proper spark, you have eliminated the lead wire and high-tension circuits as possible problems.

A SECOND APPROACH TO THE ENGINE

THE LOW-VOLTAGE CIRCUIT
CONVENTIONAL POINT SET IGNITION

Now it is time to test the low-voltage circuit and make distinctions.

Open the distributor and rotate the engine until the points are open. Leave the ignition switch in the On position. Get out the trusty volt/ohmmeter and place the red lead on the stationary point. Place the black lead on any ground. You should read either 6 or 12 volts. Most conventional ignition systems use a resistor in the ignition circuit to reduce 12-volt current to 6 volts; some do not. Did you get a proper reading? You have current to the points. Check them for a burned, pitted or oxidized condition. If they're faulty, replace them. Use a feeler gauge to check the gap. If you have a dwell meter, that is even better. Adjust the ignition points as needed, and check the condenser on a tester. If you find any problem here, replace it.

When the points and condenser are in proper condition and adjustment, you should get your spark. But what if there was no spark available at the ignition points?

Troubleshooting Gasoline Marine Engines - John Fleming

NO FIRE AT THE POINTS

If there is no fire at the points, move backwards. The ignition switch should still be in the On position. Using the VOM, check the input lead that comes through the side of the distributor. Check the low-tension (output) side of the coil, then check the input side of the coil.

POSSIBILITIES

1. The lead wire from the coil to the points may be faulty. If there is current at the output side of the coil but none at the points, this wire is at fault.
2. The coil may be at fault. If there is current at the input side but none at the output side, the coil is faulty.
3. If there is no current at the input side, trace the wiring back to the resistor. Check both sides of the resistor. Current in but none out? Replace the resistor.
4. No current at the resistor? Check the wiring circuit and harness back to the ignition switch.
5. Wiring okay? Check input and output sides to the ignition switch. If there is current at the switch but none coming out, the switch is at fault. If there is none at the switch, move backwards towards the battery.
6. Check all leads and terminals between the ignition switch and the battery.

SUPPOSE IT ALL CHECKS OUT

Now it is time to remember that solenoid switch. On older engines, there was a conductor lead from the output side of the starter solenoid to the output side of the resistor or the input side of the ignition coil in the low-voltage ignition circuit. What did it do? When the starter solenoid was engaged, it bypassed the resistor and provided 12-volt current to the coil. This provided added spark intensity during the starting cycle.

Troubleshooting Gasoline Marine Engines - John Fleming

As soon as the switch passed from the Start mode to the Run mode, this circuit disengaged and the engine ran on 6-volt current.

An ignition switch in one of these systems does not deliver current to the ignition circuit in the Start mode. If the starter solenoid fails to deliver current to the ignition system in the Start mode, the entire system can be in otherwise-perfect condition, and you can tear your hair out looking for errors.

How to recognize this problem? Your starter is in excellent condition, and the engine turns over rapidly. It is always hard to start, but now and then as you release the starter and the ignition switch drops back to the On position, the engine will crank.

Why? The engine is already turning rapidly. It has no spark, but as the switch returns to the On position, current is restored to the ignition circuit. Suddenly a spark plug receives a spark and the engine starts. How to test for this problem? Again, use the VOM. You have already checked out the system, and when the ignition switch is in the On position, you have a spark at the input side of the ignition coil.

Place the red lead from the VOM on the input side of the coil, ground the black lead, and turn the ignition switch to On. Now turn the ignition switch to Start. If the current disappears, the solenoid is at fault.

THE LOW-VOLTAGE CIRCUIT CAPACITIVE DISCHARGE ELECTRONIC IGNITION

The parts of this system are:

1. A 12 -volt coil
2. An electronic module
3. A special magnetic-distributor rotor

Troubleshooting Gasoline Marine Engines - John Fleming

HOW IT WORKS

The low-voltage circuit on a capacitive-discharge ignition system is quite simple. It consists of a 12-volt coil and a control module, which is quite small and located on the distributor plate. This module contains a capacitor which receives current from the battery, amplifies and stores it. Also inside the module is a transistor which serves as a switch. It replaces the ignition points in the conventional system. There is a rotor which encircles the distributor shaft, and this rotor is equipped with a magnet for each cylinder. As the magnet passes the electronic module, it trips the transistor and allows the capacitor to discharge through the coil.

REPAIRS TO THE CAPACITIVE DISCHARGE SYSTEM

You can not repair an electronic module; you can only replace it. The life of this part is about 750 hours. The clues that may suggest its failure are:

1. Its age, if known
2. The availability of current at the module leads, but no spark out
3. A lack of continuity. Remove the leads from the coil, set the VOM on Resistance and check for continuity.
4. Results of a test for function on an electronic tester

The module costs about $60, and I carry a spare on my boat at all times. If I'm on the water and my engine loses its spark, I begin by making visual and preliminary checks as described above. If I believe I have narrowed the problem down to the module but can not be certain, I simply replace the suspect module as a means of checking it out. There are complete testing systems available for all types of conventional and electronic ignition systems and magnetos. All come with

Troubleshooting Gasoline Marine Engines - John Fleming

detailed instructions. If you own one, you should certainly employ them.

The methods described in this chapter will help categorize and isolate engine problems more rapidly, and if you're not so lucky as to have the proper test equipment, they may salvage a fishing trip. They could also save your life.

Troubleshooting Gasoline Marine Engines - John Fleming

Troubleshooting Gasoline Marine Engines - John Fleming

CHAPTER FOUR
TEST THE FUEL SYSTEM

The engine turns over on the starter and has an excellent blue/white spark. We're now ready to consider the possibility that fuel may be the cause of difficulties. In this chapter we will run through the operation of the fuel system and search it for malfunction.

THE PARTS OF THE FUEL SYSTEM

1. The fuel tank
2. A fuel supply
3. A pickup (bayonet) tube to retrieve fuel from the tank
4. A shutoff valve at the top of the tank
5. A set of fuel lines
6. A fuel filter
7. A fuel pump
8. A carburetor

HOW IT SHOULD WORK

The engine turns over and the camshaft operates a fulcrum on the fuel pump. The diaphragm in the pump is forced up and down, and it draws a vacuum on the fuel line. This draws fuel from the bayonet pickup tube in the fuel tank through the shutoff valve and through the fuel filter into its

Troubleshooting Gasoline Marine Engines - John Fleming

own body. The fuel pump then pressurizes that fuel and delivers it to the carburetor inlet. The fuel passes through the inlet valve and into the carburetor bowl. From this point it is available for delivery to the engine through either the jets or the accelerator pump.

HOW TO TEST THIS SYSTEM

Begin at the end of the line at the carburetor. Start by removing the spark arrestor atop the carburetor. If the engine is cold, the choke butterfly should be closed. If the engine is warm, the butterfly should be in the open position.

Get an assistant to operate the throttle through one or two cycles. Open and close, open and close. You should see a healthy stream of fuel discharged from the dump tubes into the carburetor venturi. If you do not, your trouble is a lack of fuel.

If there is sufficient fuel to make a healthy stream but the choke butterflies are not in their assigned positions, you may have a flooded or starving engine. Open butterflies on a cold engine will starve it. Closed butterflies on a hot engine will flood it. Are the butterflies in the proper position? Still no fuel? Pull the coil wire out of the distributor and ground it solidly on the cylinder head. By doing so you preclude any spark. Take the appropriate wrench and remove the fuel line from the inlet side of the carburetor. Hold a jar under the fuel line and turn the engine over with the starter. Did you get a solid stream of fuel?

If you got plenty of fuel out of the pump but none going to the carburetor, the inlet valve in the carburetor is stuck, or the small filter on the side of the carburetor is plugged. No fuel at the pump? Replace the line at the carburetor and move back to the intake side of the fuel pump.

Using the same hand-operated evacuation pump that you employ to drain your crankcase, pull a vacuum on this line. Did you get any fuel? Did the flow come easily? You have a faulty fuel pump. How about no fuel at the intake? Replace the

Troubleshooting Gasoline Marine Engines - John Fleming

fuel line and move back to the filter. Check the bowl for contamination. Any water in the fuel, sediment in the bowl or leaks at the lines? Everything okay? Remove the fuel line from the inlet side of the fuel filter. Using the same pump, draw a vacuum on the fuel line (on the tank-side of the filter). If you get fuel here, the filter is somehow at fault. Go back through the last checks, remove the filter element and check for contamination. Did you fail to get fuel at the tank line? Replace all hoses and fuel lines.

Go back to the shut-off valve and remove the fuel line from the valve. Remove the valve and hold it in your hands. Set it into the open position and cover the open end with a finger. Try to create pressure or draw a vacuum on this valve with your mouth. (This is no fun, but it is a good check.) The valve leaks? Replace it.

The valve feels good? Attach the vacuum pump to the fuel tank outlet and apply a vacuum to the bayonet pickup. If you get fuel here, you know that, regardless of how hard you tried, you did not detect the problem with the fuel shutoff valve. Replace it.

If you do not get fuel at this point, there are three possibilities:

1. The bayonet pickup has broken inside the tank and has fallen down.
2. The bayonet pickup has become clogged and can not pass fuel.
3. You're out of gasoline.

You should have found the problem with your fuel supply by now. Remember that you have grounded the coil lead, so go back and restore it to its proper place. The engine should crank.

Troubleshooting Gasoline Marine Engines - John Fleming

CHECKS TO MAKE AT STARTUP

Suppose the engine does crank. Always check your exhaust discharge for water flow when the engine first starts. If you have someone else available to do this, it is most convenient, but the operator should be responsible. Look at the exhaust discharge.

With the engine running, there is more to be learned. Does the exhaust smoke? If so, is it blue or black? Black smoke coming from the exhaust means a very rich mixture. You need not be terribly impressed if you see a bit of black smoke for a few minutes after the engine starts. It may go on for a short time, but only until the choke is released. But if it continues, you have carburetor problems. These may not be serious enough to stop the engine, but they will waste fuel, affect the idle, and one day the plugs will foul. Then the engine will not start.

Suppose the smoke is blue or gray? This means the engine is burning oil. It may be coming down through the valve-stem seals or leaking upwards through the oil-control rings, but blue/gray smoke is a bad sign.

Another worthwhile check is for coolant in a heat exchanger if one is installed. With the engine running, remove the filler cap. If there are bubbles present, watch carefully. Do they continue to form over several minutes? If so, you probably have internal problems in the engine. A blown head gasket, a cracked valve seat, a cracked cylinder head: any of these will cause bubbles. It is time for a compression check. A clue: does the engine ever run hot, or does it have a history of doing so? You may have found the cause.

Remember, we're not trying to fine-tune this engine. At this point we seek only to get under way. The steps outlined in the first four chapters are emergency procedures only. Those listed under the Checks to Make at Start-Up section are intended to indicate additional steps you may need to take later. If you're a mechanic or a mechanically inclined

Troubleshooting Gasoline Marine Engines - John Fleming

individual, you will realize that much remains to be done if the engine is to be fully addressed.

Somewhere within the several processes described in these four chapters lies 85 percent of the problems that cause the marine engine to fail to start. Study them carefully, and no matter how tiresome the reading may be, savor the knowledge. It will serve you well.

Troubleshooting Gasoline Marine Engines - John Fleming

CHAPTER FIVE
THE TUNE-UP

I'll begin this chapter on the assumption that the engine is running but has some failings. It skips, it surges, it loses power, or suffers any of several maladies. We're going to try to tune up this baby.

THE COMPRESSION CHECK

I start every tune-up, whether on a conventional or electronic engine, with a compression check. This uses about 20 minutes and costs about as many dollars in the present economy, and it is worth every penny. Here is a truism that you can take to the bank: You can not tune an engine with low or no compression. Try as you might, it will not work.

What are the parameters? There are two checks, one for the maximum numbers, the other for balance. For the first check, the cylinders should be within 15 percent of new pressures. Compare the maximum cylinder pressures shown by the compression gauge to those provided for new engines by the service manual. The difference should be no more than 15 percent on any cylinder.

For the second check, compare the cylinder with the highest compression reading to that of the cylinder with the lowest. There should be no more than 15 pounds variation between the highest and lowest readings. If either reading is outside allowable specifications, you have a problem.

Troubleshooting Gasoline Marine Engines - John Fleming

HOW TO RUN THE COMPRESSION CHECK

First remove all the spark plugs. We're ready to begin a paper outline. Place the plugs on a sheet of paper, which will become the outline. Lay them out in the order in which they came from the engine and in the same configuration as the alignment of the cylinder block.

Why is this important? Certain cylinders are closer and certain cylinders farther from the carburetor. There is a natural tendency for those remote cylinders to run leaner than the cylinders positioned closer to the carburetor. These situations should become obvious from the paper outline

Open the throttle wide, remove the coil lead, and ground it to the cylinder head. If the throttle is closed while you take compression readings, they will be universally low. Now screw a compression gauge into the spark plug hole and turn the engine over for three rotations. Repeat this procedure with each successive cylinder. Try to turn each cylinder the same number of times. This provides a more consistent reading. Write down the readings beside the spark plug from the cylinder you're testing. The spark plugs will help to reinforce those readings and help interpret the results. Inspect the plugs carefully before you proceed.

WHAT DO THE NUMBERS MEAN?

Full compression on all cylinders means that the engine has a good set of compression rings. The insulators on the spark plugs should be a light gray or orange color, with little or no residue on the body of the plugs.

Even compression between cylinders, coupled with the proper reading in Paragraph One, means that the engine has good valves, good compression rings, and the head gaskets are sealing. You can proceed with the tune-up.

Troubleshooting Gasoline Marine Engines - John Fleming

LOW-COMPRESSION PROBLEMS

If the compression reading is low, what then? The answer lies in the answers to two questions — how low is the reading, and are all cylinders equally low? If so, the engine is showing its age. The valves still seal, but the compression rings are worn. To assure yourself of this, add two squirts of oil to each cylinder and repeat the compression test. The numbers should improve dramatically as the oil seals the rings. A 50 lbs./in./sq/ or greater change is a sure sign that your piston rings are failing. If those readings are consistent across all the cylinders, you will still be able to achieve a fairly good tune-up but you will not be able to restore full power. You can proceed with the tune-up, but be warned that this engine has problems and is reaching a critical stage in its life. An overhaul will be reasonably priced now, yet it may be very expensive later.

Suppose the engine has low compression on one or more cylinders but higher readings on others. Now we wish to look at distribution. Two adjacent cylinders with a lower reading probably have a head gasket blown between the two. A single cylinder or scattered cylinders with low readings may mean a blown head gasket or burned valves.

If the numbers are low enough, zero or near-zero, they could also indicate a failed piston. It is desirable to learn all that you can about the engine before you begin to tear it down, but those very low or erratic readings can only be cured in one manner. The head(s) are coming off at the very least. (The tear-down is reserved for another chapter.) Let us go back to the earlier assumption that the compression readings are good, so proceed from there.

GOOD COMPRESSION

Up to this point, everything I have described is the procedure I follow regardless of whether the engine employs fuel injection or what ignition system is used. From this point,

Troubleshooting Gasoline Marine Engines - John Fleming

we will proceed differently according to the type of engine.

For full electronic engines, revert to the laptop and a service manual. You really should not attempt to address these engines without the proper test equipment. For others it is a good idea to look at the spark plugs. They can help to aim you in the proper direction.

Spark plugs tell a story in cylinders with both good and bad compression. This portion of our text deals with cylinders with good compression, so we will expect to see an insulator that has a gray or light-orange coloring.

1. If the color is dark gray, you're probably burning oil
2. If the insulator is white, your mixture may be too lean
3. If the insulator is black, your mixture may be too rich
4. If the body of the plug and the insulator are both wet, wipe the residue on your finger. Feel and smell the residue for gasoline or oily content. The presence of wet gasoline indicates a flooded engine
5. The presence of oil indicates failed oil-control rings or leaky valve-stem seals
6. Good compression rings do not necessarily indicate good oil control rings

There are other symptoms that may be recognized from spark plug insulators. The presence of excessive gap indicates long usage. Blisters on the insulator indicate excessive heat. The engine may be running lean, the spark timing may be too far advanced, the fuel octane rating may be too low, or the heat range of the spark plugs may be excessive.

The presence of small aluminum beads on the insulator is bad news indeed. These are minuscule parts of your pistons! This too can be caused by all of those things listed in the last paragraph but simply carried to great extremes. If you see these beads on your insulators, you must discover the cause right now. Water in small drops on the insulator or rust on the plug body are another bad sign. Usually this indicates a failed

Troubleshooting Gasoline Marine Engines - John Fleming

head gasket, a cracked head or other even more serious problems. Look for water in the oil or a loss of coolant from the closed- circuit cooling if the engine is so equipped. Again, this problem must be addressed.

The reading of spark plug insulators is an inexact science because coloration depends to some extent upon the additives. The fuel and the coloration that we sought as good indicators when I was young are no longer valid today, so consult a spark plug chart for up-to-date coloration. If you're puzzled by what you see, you might even consult a local gasoline distributor or someone who specializes in engine tuning. After 60 years of working on engines, I still ask questions.

THE PLUGS LOOK GOOD

The plugs check out and compression is not a problem. You can proceed with your tune-up. If appropriate, talk to the engine's owner. For what reason did he/she approach you to begin with?

THE ENGINE RUNS RAGGEDLY AT ANY SPEED

It has that familiar, shaky, uneven operation up and down the rpm scale. This is generally caused by ignition and is typical of spark plug failure, ignition wire break down, etc. Go back to Chapter Three and check all of the ignition-system parts as listed. Add a check for ignition timing. Use a timing light.

THE ENGINE RUNS SMOOTHLY BUT IT SURGES

The engine will not achieve or maintain top speed. Surging generally indicates fuel problems. Install a fuel-

Troubleshooting Gasoline Marine Engines - John Fleming

pressure gauge (about $20 at the parts house) in the fuel line between the fuel inlet and the carburetor. Clean off any spilled fuel. Operate the blower, then crank the engine. Put the engine in gear, and be certain you have a clear path ahead. Run the engine at gradually increasing rpm in increments of 100. The fuel-pressure gauge should read 5 lbs/in^2 at all times. If the fuel pressure should fall below this when the engine begins to lose power, your problem is in the fuel delivery system. Check all the components listed in Chapter Four. One or more is failing in its mission. If fuel pressure remains constant and the engine runs smoothly but still loses power, the problem is probably in the carburetor. It is getting plenty of fuel but is not using it properly.

THE ENGINE DEVELOPS BLACK SMOKE IN THE EXHAUST

This is the indication of an overly rich mixture. You may be able to make some adjustments to the carburetor without removing it from the manifold, but I never do this unless I'm in an emergency situation. It is better to remove and boil the carburetor, install an overhaul kit, and flow the carburetor on a flow bench if possible.

THE ENGINE USES TOO MUCH FUEL

The answer may lie in the general tune-up recommended in steps two and three, but the problem can also be caused by a propeller with too much diameter or pitch. Retarded ignition timing is also a possibility.

A clogged spark arrestor can cause the engine to consume too much fuel. In fact. a badly clogged spark arrestor can draw enough fuel to wash the cylinders with raw fuel and cause early engine failure. Any tune-up should include washing and cleaning this accessory. If the arrestor is heavily clogged, this is usually the result of crankcase blow-by. Burned gases

Troubleshooting Gasoline Marine Engines - John Fleming

are escaping around the compression rings, entering the crankcase and carrying residue through the positive crankcase vent to the arrestor. You must find out why. In fact, it is almost inconceivable that you will find this condition and yet not discover the cause during the compression check. You might need to check those figures again. A thorough tune-up for any marine engine actually anticipates the complete analysis and potential replacement of any or all those parts listed in the fuel and ignition systems. (I also use tune-up time as an excuse to quickly examine other parts of the engine.)

A quick visual inspection of all liquid levels, all belts and their tension adjustment or any visible oil leaks is appropriate at this time. Tune-up time is also a fine excuse to review the maintenance interval. Is the engine nearly due for an oil and filter change? Why not combine the two and save the added down-time?

There is a tune-up procedure described in every service manual, and it is always a good idea to own one. Yet the foregoing chapter offers a pretty good insight into the process, regardless of whether you own the exact publication for your particular powerplant.

From this point forward, the recommended procedures are appropriate for all engines. They apply regardless of fuel or ignition system.

Troubleshooting Gasoline Marine Engines - John Fleming

CHAPTER SIX
LOW COMPRESSION
HOW TO PROCEED

Assume you have found low compression on one or more cylinders. How do you proceed? That depends on the sequence and location of the cylinders with the poor readings. Let us try a variety of possibilities and look at each in turn for potential remedies. We will consider the thorough and proper approach as well as minimally acceptable remedies. Not all boat owners will want to spend the money for complete repairs, regardless of the implications of a lesser approach.

COMPRESSION IS LOW BUT EVEN ON ALL CYLINDERS

This indicates an engine with advanced hours. It is wearing evenly and properly, but the valves no longer seat perfectly and the compression rings have lost some of their seal. You can probably tune this engine to give a smooth idle, but you will never restore full power or fuel economy without an overhaul. If the total compression figures are 20 percent or more below new, you should begin seriously considering a tear-down. At this time you may get by with rings, bearings and a valve grind. If you continue to run the engine, you will surely require pistons and a bore job. In extreme cases, the blow-by on your piston rings may heat a connecting rod and destroy the crankshaft.

This is the discretionary engine that we described in the opening paragraph. The owner has to look this problem squarely in the face and decide where to go with it. Fix it now, or patch and pray. That is the choice.

COMPRESSION IS LOW FOR ONE OR MORE CYLINDERS

If the difference is more than 15 pounds, you have either burned a valve, blown a head gasket, cracked a valve seat, or some other part of the engine has failed. The answer lies inside the engine.

Figure 3
John Fleming

Water penetration into the cylinders is a common problem. Check carefully for the signs.

If the spark plug from one of those low-compression cylinders has water on the insulator or rust on the plug base, it can help reinforce your analysis. Yet, the lack of these indicators does not negate the remedy required. There is little

Troubleshooting Gasoline Marine Engines - John Fleming

value in speculation or trying for an exact diagnosis from outside the engine. (It has to come apart anyway.)

At the very least you will need to remove the head(s) so the diagnosis will be easier. The procedures for testing after the head is off are best done by a competent machine shop. They include testing the heads to be certain that the sealing surfaces are straight (within .002 inch across the face), checking the valve seats for cracks (die or other test), and the top of the cylinder block (deck) for straightness (again .002).

On a V-6 or V-8 engine, if the low-compression figures show up on one cylinder bank only, you may not need to pull the other head.

THE ENGINE RUNS ROUGH - A COMPRESSION GAUGE ISN'T AVAILABLE

First crank the engine. Using a pair of insulated pliers, pull the wires off the spark plugs one at a time. If the engine slows down, this cylinder is firing and pulling to some degree. If the engine does not slow down, you have at least isolated the problem to a particular cylinder. You may want to alternately remove and replace the wire several times. Listen carefully to the engine; some cylinders will affect the engine more than others.

With practice you will be able to tell which cylinders are pulling hardest, which have some problems, and which are totally dead. Low compression is not necessarily the culprit in this test. Other problems could cause a weak or dead cylinder. At least you have a place to start.

THE HEADS ARE OFF

Look at the cylinder head gasket. Did you have two side-by-side cylinders with low compression? The gasket sealing rings should be very dark at the narrow junction between them. Look at the areas where the gasket seals around the water passages. Are there any dark areas between the water passage and the cylinder bore? The engine may have been pulling water from the cooling system. If it tended to run hot, you have at least found a part of the problem. Is the gasket heavily burned or missing parts in some areas? This is generally a sign of detonation. The engine is running high timing, or the gasoline does not have a sufficient octane rating. Overloads or oversize propellers will also cause this. Is the gasket blown in a number of places all around the cylinder head? This is generally caused by one of the problems in the preceding paragraph.

HIGH-PERFORMANCE ENGINES

It is possible to detect a few additional signs. For instance, assume the outside two cylinders on a four-cylinder bank have blown their head gasket. These cylinders are farthest from the carburetor. The center cylinders receive the fuel first, and thus they tend to run richer. If the plugs from the outside cylinders alone show signs of heat and the gasket is blown, you're getting detonation. Consult an expert in speed tuning and save yourself some grief. I have seen a hard-headed mechanic replace a head gasket four times under these conditions, before the engine let go.

MORE ABOUT HIGH-PERFORMANCE ENGINES

Screw the spark plugs from failed cylinders back into the head and torque down the plugs on a new gasket. Are the threads from the base of the plug extending into the cylinder head? You can not afford even a single thread. The sharp edges of those threads become glow plugs at high speed and cause pre-ignition. What to do? Make a set of shims from brass stock on your lathe. Fit them to each cylinder, and always keep the shims with the proper cylinder when changing plugs. I have

Troubleshooting Gasoline Marine Engines - John Fleming

not torn down a single stock engine or removed a cylinder head from any factory product that did not have this problem to some degree, or even to an embarrassing extent, in the past 30 years.

READING A HEAD GASKET

This is a bit like reading spark plugs, an inexact science at which you will become more adept with practice. Every time you see an engine disassembled in any shop, ask to see the head gasket. After asking what caused the problems prompting the tear-down, look carefully at that gasket and see if you can pick out the indications of the problems described to you. If the mechanic who disassembled the engine is known to be very good at his job, ask him to show you the indicators on the gaskets. This is one of the surest ways to get a good education in reading the signs written across a head gasket. You have cause and effect in an easy-to-observe setting, and you did not even have to turn a wrench!

I'll close this chapter with a few generalizations. First, I do not believe in using regular (87 octane) gasoline in an engine with compression ratios above 8-3/4. Even when the manufacturer recommends this fuel, there is too much difference between fuels sold at the various locations, and it is too easy to slip over the line on engine loading.

Also, the laboratory and the sea are two separate environs. Engines are tuned very close to the edge for the sake of economy and pollution control, but it is easy to cross over that edge one day when the boater faces unexpected conditions.

For instance, you're called upon to render assistance to a disabled vessel, and though the seas are high, you can hardly refuse. If you respond and take another vessel under tow, your engine is history. (I consider a compression ratio of 8-3/4:1, naturally aspirated, at the extreme edge for low-octane fuels.)

Troubleshooting Gasoline Marine Engines - John Fleming

Troubleshooting Gasoline Marine Engines - John Fleming

CHAPTER SEVEN
VISUAL SIGNS

I'm a great believer in using the eyes; the engine tells us many things that can be learned from observation alone. The good mechanic is always alert for any of these signs and may add to his/her income to a considerable degree by making appropriate observations. Surely the boater can benefit from the same exercise. What am I looking for? Let us begin with the obvious signs and then move on to the more subtle indicators.

OIL IN THE BILGES

Look at the surface of the engine. Do you see oil leaking around the rocker covers? This may only be a faulty gasket. If so, it should be replaced. It can also indicate heavy blow-by or a plugged positive crankcase ventilation (PCV) valve. Check the breather and the PCV system.

Is oil coming down from the top of the rocker covers? You may need a new grommet to seal the PCV valve where it is installed into the rocker cover. Do you have leakage from the other side of the engine? Maybe the oil filler cap is leaking.

Oil coming from the top of the dipstick tube can also mean excessive blow-by. Oil coming from the bottom of the engine should be traced to the source. Is it coming from the filter body? It may be a bad gasket. Do not forget there is a gasket between the cylinder block and the filter mounting base.

That sometimes fails also.

Look at the flywheel cover and the bottom of the bell housing. Oil at this point indicates a leaking seal at the rear main bearing. These seals may leak only a drop now and then, and while this is not desirable, it is also not destructive. Keep the bilge clean and watch the leak.

If the leak becomes excessive, you may have a worn or failed rear main seal and it must be replaced. This is a real problem because there is no way to reach/replace it without removing the transmission, drive plate and flywheel. Engines manufactured after 1986 have the seal mounted on the outside of the cylinder block, and the seals can be replaced without removing the crankcase pan. On older engines with internal rope seals, you will have to pull the engine and remove the pan to get to the seal. Any time a rear main seal fails, there is the possibility that it was caused by a worn or failed rear main bearing. On any engine I first determine if there is an obvious reason for the seal to fail. If I can not find such a sign, I prefer to check the rear main bearing. There is some reason why the seal failed, and if that reason is not apparent from outside, it almost surely is inside the engine.

THE PROBLEM MAY NOT BE THE MAIN BEARING SEAL

A freeze plug covers the rear camshaft bearing, and it sits in a machined circular hole in the block. There are instances when it has rusted through or otherwise failed. If you replace it, always use a brass plug. No one likes to tear into an engine at a cost of many dollars because a $10 seal or a $3 steel plug rusted through.

LOOK AT THE EXHAUST MANIFOLDS

Is there evidence of corrosion at the elbow joints or gaskets? This is indicated by a white line around the gasket

Troubleshooting Gasoline Marine Engines - John Fleming

where salt corrosion is bleeding out or by a few beads of rust running down the pipes. You want to replace these gaskets at the first sign of rust or corrosion. That pipe runs right back into your cylinder heads, and if it leaks to the outside, it almost surely leaks to the inside. Untold numbers of good engines have been destroyed by leaking exhaust manifolds. Valves and pistons are among the parts that are hostage to this seal.

LOOK FOR RUST AROUND THE FRONT OF THE ENGINE

A leaking water pump will sling water all over the front part of the engine. You will have to check both the circulating pump and the raw-water pump because either may be the culprit in this instance. Both are located at the front of the engine, and a leak from either can be destructive. Water thrown into alternators will certainly cause them to fail. Water deposited on pulleys and belts will cause both to fail. Water thrown on the front of the engine can cause the timing cover to leak through or the pan to do the same.

LOOK FOR RUST ON THE SIDES OF THE BLOCK

There are freeze plugs on the side of the block that can develop a leak. If they do, they should be replaced. This is a simple procedure, and it can save the cosmetics on the engine.

IS THE ENGINE EQUIPPED WITH FRESHWATER (CLOSED-CIRCUIT) COOLING?

Look for corrosion around the end caps on the heat exchanger. Leaking gaskets or seals should be replaced. The leaks will be indicated by a water residue during operation or any signs of corrosion. While you're looking at the heat exchanger, you may want to check the zinc pencil anode for wear. When this anode is 25 percent gone, it is 100 percent ineffective, so replace it. The anode costs a couple of bucks; that heat exchanger costs several hundreds.

LOOK FOR DARK COLORATION AT THE SPARK ARRESTOR

Generally this is an indication of blow-by and always an indication that the arrestor should be cleaned. I do this frequently as a maintenance item. The presence of any dark coloration is a warning sign.

WHILE THE SPARK ARRESTOR IS OFF

Check the carburetor venturis for color. You should see a clean aluminum coloration. If you have oily or greasy-black residue coupled with a clogged or semi-clogged spark arrestor, this indicates extreme blow-by.

If the carburetor venturis are dry but blackened, you're probably losing one or more valves. The intake valves are leaking burned gases back through the intake manifold and into the carburetor during high-speed operation. Your compression gauge will probably confirm this.

Another possibility is floating cam followers (lifters). The cam followers are either pumping up (hydraulic lifters) or floating (solid lifters). This can be from excessive rpm or poor valve springs, but regardless of the source of the problem, you must correct it. A blackened venturi in the carburetor is not good news.

Troubleshooting Gasoline Marine Engines - John Fleming

CONSIDER APPEARANCE

A clean, well-maintained engine is a joy to own, and almost every mariner or mechanic looks at the cosmetics before anything else. When you open the engine room on a clean and well-painted powerplant, you generally make a lasting impression on any observer. If you're the mechanic who services the engine, you will also be remembered for your efforts. Both the owner and the mechanic benefit from a clean engine. The Coast Guard seldom fails to notice as well. Your boarding officer will give you brownie points for cleanliness belowdecks.

Troubleshooting Gasoline Marine Engines - John Fleming

Troubleshooting Gasoline Marine Engines - John Fleming

CHAPTER EIGHT
AUDIBLE SIGNALS

Sound tells us a great deal about the engine, but before you can use this knowledge, you must first learn to differentiate, to separate parts of a sound from the overall din. For many years I was a captain on oil field vessels. When I first went aboard a crew boat, I quickly realized that the captain who was to train me could lie in a bunk and sleep soundly at night, even though the VHF radio was operating continuously and a generator was making loud noises.

There were literally dozens of calls on that radio, mostly ignored, but if the rig called for the MV Cirrhus, the captain was instantly awake. I did not believe I'd ever be able to differentiate between those calls in the dead of night while sleeping soundly. It was less than a week before I could do so easily. The sounds of a running engine are like those that I heard on that crew boat, lo those many years ago. There are numerous noisy little messages passing back and forth, hidden in the overall cacophony of engine sounds, and in time you will learn to differentiate between each of them.

A valve tap or cam follower is the lightest of the danger signals. A loose wrist pin has a deeper noise. Next in line is the worn connecting-rod bearing, followed by the worn main bearing. Each of these problems has an increasingly deeper tone. Experience will aid you in trying to determine which of these you're hearing.

Happily, there are other ways to do this as well. For the next few paragraphs we will assume the engine is equipped

Troubleshooting Gasoline Marine Engines - John Fleming

with hydraulic lifters. That light tap you're hearing is probably excessive valve lash. We know hydraulic tappets run on zero lash and that they should make very little or no noise at all. What do you do? Remove the rocker cover. With the engine running at idle, place you fingers on the rocker arms alternately. You will easily be able to feel the slack and tapping rocker arm. You can try adjusting the lash out of the offending member if you wish, and there is a small chance that you can do so.

Once you have established that there is excessive lash in the valve train, you will almost certainly have to remove the intake manifold and check out the system. The parts involved are:

1. The camshaft
2. The cam follower (lifter)
3. The pushrod
4. The rocker arm
5. The mounting ball for the rocker arm
6. The valve spring(s)
7. The valve spring retainer
8. The valve
9. The valve-stem locks
10. The rocker stud

PROBLEMS AND REMEDIES

1. The camshaft lobes are worn. Replace the camshaft.
2. The lifter is stuck. Replace it.
3. The push rod is worn on the ends. Replace it.
4. The rocker arm is worn. Replace it.
5. The rocker-arm mounting ball is worn. Replace it.
6. Put the valve spring/s on a spring compression tester and check for tension. Replace if needed.
7. Valve stems
8. Valve spring retainers

Troubleshooting Gasoline Marine Engines - John Fleming

9. Retainer locks. Consider #7, #8 and #9 together as one group. Few problems ever arise with these parts, but when they do, all are usually involved. If the retainers and locks are loose or missing, the valve stem is usually damaged also. This will probably require removal of the cylinder head.

10. The rocker stud is loose. On occasion, the rocker stud may be jacked out of its mounting socket in the cylinder head. This usually requires removal of the head and a screw-in or pinned stud. This is a job for the machine shop. You can remove and replace the head.

The steps involved in numbers 1 through 6 can be accomplished on the engine. Get a spark plug and remove all of the insulation from the base. Braze or weld a short pipe nipple into the top of the base, and screw an air lug to the nipple. Install the spark plug into the faulty cylinder, and attach a high-pressure air hose to the lug. Use about 100 lbs./in^2. to 125 lbs./in.^{2}. air pressure on the cylinder. That will easily support the valve in position while you work on it. Remove the carburetor, rocker cover and intake manifold. This will give access to the cam shaft. the followers and the parts of the valve train. A service manual will describe in detail the full procedure for a given engine.

THE SOUND HAS A DEEPER RESONANCE

This is probably a wrist pin or connecting-rod bearing. If the knock is truly deep-toned, it may be a main bearing. It is not really important which, since each of these problems requires that the engine be disassembled.

How can you determine whether you have a problem with wrist pins or bearings? Run the engine at idle. Using insulated pliers, remove the spark plug leads one at a time and replace them. The engine should develop a louder tap or knock on the affected cylinder.

What's happening? The piston is moving up and down.

Troubleshooting Gasoline Marine Engines - John Fleming

So long as there is compression on the piston top, it tends to keep the slack out, and the engine does not knock so loudly. Release that plug wire, the engine ceases to fire, and the knocking becomes more severe, the sound louder.

Another check will also detect bearings with a lesser amount of wear that are just beginning to sound off. Using a large, heavy screwdriver, place the blade against the cylinder head near the spark plug hole. Now wrap your hand around the handle, leaving a small amount of space between the end of the handle and your thumb. This small pocket forms a sound chamber. Place your ear against the side of your thumb and encircle the ear with thumb and forefinger. You will be amazed what you can hear. Parts houses manufacture a kind of stethoscope for this purpose, and it works very well, but if you do not have one, the screwdriver trick is very good.

Will you really know what you're hearing? Maybe not at first. Listen to each cylinder, one at a time. They will sound slightly different, but you will be able to detect a considerable difference in the sounds coming from a really faulty cylinder.

Do not arbitrarily tear the engine down based upon this evidence alone if you have never used this method before. Get some good advice from someone familiar with the system. Check the results you perceive, as compared to the results described by an experienced practitioner. In time you will become most proficient at interpreting the sounds of the running engine.

Here's another suggestion: Try the screwdriver stethoscope on every engine you encounter, even new ones and especially those in various age categories. Soon they'll talk to you in a language you can easily understand. Combine the above checks. With spark-plug wire detached, cylinder without fire, the screwdriver stethoscope will really speak out.

GRINDING SOUNDS

Generally these are ball bearings gone berserk. They can be expected at the front of the engine, and they come from

Troubleshooting Gasoline Marine Engines - John Fleming

circulating water pumps, raw-water pumps or alternator bearings. They can even come from all three at once.

You must learn to combine the techniques described in these chapters. Do you remember the earlier description of an engine with rust spread across the front and the probable cause? A faulty water pump? Water is flying everywhere from a failed seal. It is not likely that all the bearings would fail simultaneously, but if one of the accessories is throwing saltwater into all of them, there is a possibility they might.

THE GRIND CAN BE INTERNAL

The timing chain is seldom heard on the engine, even when it is ready to fail. The timing gear is another matter. The opposite-rotation engine has a gear-driven camshaft that can sometimes make a pretty good amount of noise at the front of the engine. If you have checked all of your bearings at the front of an opposite-rotation engine and they all good but the sound persists, you may have a timing gear going out.

Always be thorough in your inspections. If you're not in a patient mood, go fetch a beverage of some sort.

SQUEAKS AND SQUEALS

These are usually from the water pump and accessory drive belts at the front of the engine, but occasionally a ball bearing in the earliest stage of failure will make a rather high-pitched squeal. Begin by checking drive belts, their condition and their tension.

If this fails to produce an answer, check the bearings. Before you tear into any accessory, remove the drive belt and crank the engine. Let it run for only a moment (15 to 30 seconds) because it is not getting any cooling water. Remember, you first checked the belt and its tension as in the above paragraph, and you have eliminated the belt as the problem. If the sound disappears when the engine runs with the

Troubleshooting Gasoline Marine Engines - John Fleming

accessories at rest, the problem lies with one of those accessories.

Always be certain you have done a good job of eliminating the belt before proceeding. Elimination is a step-by-step operation in which each step is effective only if the prior operation was done correctly. This is true in all troubleshooting.

YOU TURN THE SWITCH KEY AND HEAR A SOUND, BUT THE ENGINE DOESN'T TURN OVER

Several possibilities exist:
1. The starter motor turns over rapidly but doesn't engage the flywheel.
2. The starter motor turns over slowly but doesn't engage the flywheel.
3. The starter motor turns over and produces a grinding sound, but the engine doesn't rotate.

Approach these one at a time. If the starter motor spins rapidly but doesn't engage the flywheel, it is usually the fault of the bendix. The starter has power, but the bendix has frozen. Perhaps it has a broken spring. You will have to remove the starter to remedy this. If the starter motor turns over slowly, there are three possibilities. The battery may be low, the starter itself may be in the early stages of failure, or the engine may have internal problems. The first two are the more likely. First, check the battery for charge, then examine the starter thoroughly before approaching the possibility of a tight engine.

What if the starter turns over rapidly, producing a loud grinding sound but does not engage the flywheel? You may be missing one or more teeth in the starter ring on the flywheel. If there is only one tooth gone, the engine may turn over but produce a periodic clunk as the missing tooth rotates into position.

Troubleshooting Gasoline Marine Engines - John Fleming

If several teeth are missing, the engine may fail to rotate at all, but the flying bendix gear will perhaps touch a tooth or a part of one, and the sound can scare the uninitiated.

There are other sounds that you will learn in time to differentiate between. For instance, piston slap in a worn engine makes a distinctive sound, and of course there are others. Yet you have the most common sounds listed above. Only time will really teach you to interpret those sounds, and even the most practiced mechanic occasionally calls them wrong.

Match the sounds and their probable cause to the results of your compression test and your spark plug readings. The more indicators you employ, the more accurate will be your diagnosis. Each time a new indicator matches and falls into place, your confidence in the diagnosis will increase.

Troubleshooting Gasoline Marine Engines - John Fleming

Troubleshooting Gasoline Marine Engines - John Fleming

CHAPTER NINE
THE WIRING HARNESS

The wiring harness encircles your engine like a serpentine monster. It carries electrical current to appointed places while operating in an always-moist and sometimes-greasy but forever-hostile environment. Its insulation is abraded, shaken and attacked from many directions, yet it goes without notice, serving quietly and valiantly for many years.

Several things you should know about the wiring harness. There are actually two harnesses on a standard wiring system. The on-board or engine harness is mounted on the engine and serves all its electrical functions. The panel harness connects the engine to the instrument panel, the ignition switch, etc. The two harnesses are tied together by a plug, and the male connection is usually included with the panel harness. The female connection is generally mounted rigidly on some type of bracket in a prominent place aboard the engine.

THE PROPER USE OF A WIRING DIAGRAM

Before you approach any wiring problem, first learn how to read a wiring diagram. Tracing the circuits should be a simple task. The wiring is color-coded, the diagram specifies both wire color and diameter, and thus the circuit should be easy to follow.

Somewhat less obvious may be the symbols which

Troubleshooting Gasoline Marine Engines - John Fleming

represent various switches, relays, solenoids or other appliances that also appear. It is these symbols with which you may not be familiar. If you're about to concern yourself with a wiring circuit, be certain you understand what those symbols represent. Practice on an engine, and see if you can locate them. As you trace the wiring circuit on the diagram, you can also trace it on the engine. The symbols become milestones on the way, telling you when you're on the right path.

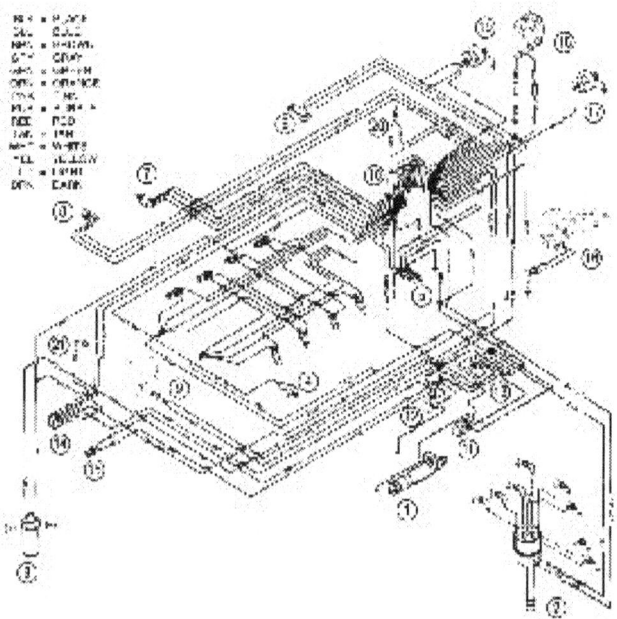

Figure 4
Courtesy of Mercury Marine

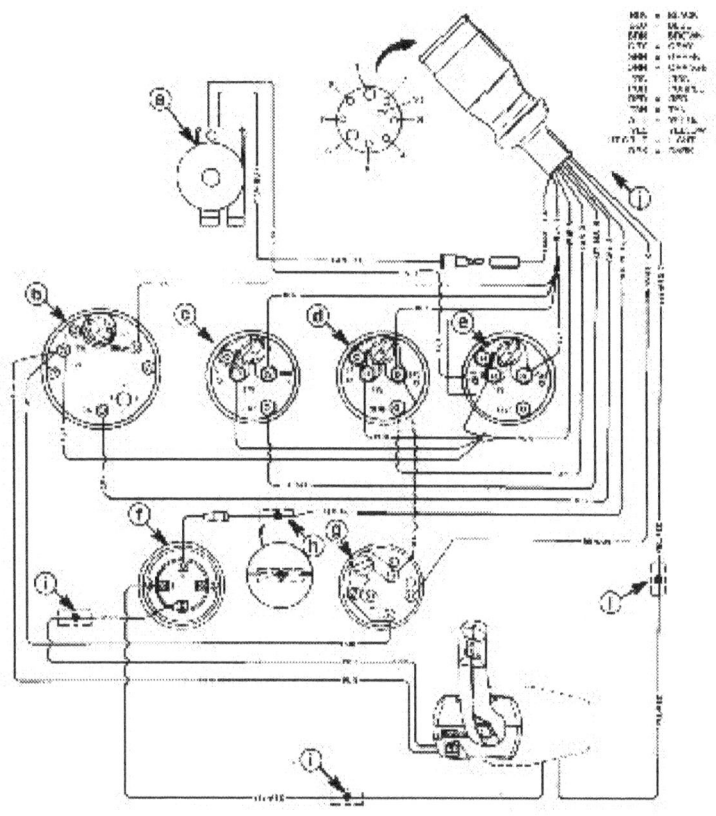

Figure 5
Courtesy of Mercury Marine

Figure 4 shows a typical engine wiring diagram. Figure 5 shows ignition switch and gauge wiring.

Some parts of the harness are coded according to a standard marine system, and I'll list them. Others are decided by the particular manufacturer, and you can not rely on your memory for these.

There are other reasons not to trust your memory. Occasionally, some misbegotten creature has cut into a harness and replaced the conductor with whatever piece of stray wire he could find. In some cases you may be faced with entire

Troubleshooting Gasoline Marine Engines - John Fleming

engines wired with a hodgepodge of wire that looks like a nightmare. A nightmare is what it is, and if you're not careful, you can make some real problems out of this situation. For now, let us assume you have familiarized yourself with the procedure for reading a wiring diagram and proceed accordingly.

RECOGNIZING A CIRCUIT

The standard wiring diagram for a marine engine employs the following recognized format:

1. Red or orange: These are hot or positive (+) leads
2. Black: These are ground or negative (-) leads

You should approach all wiring circuits with great care because a positive lead on a negative post can lead to all kinds of misery.

1. White: usually an ignition wire
2. Gray: usually a tachometer lead
3. Green: usually the oil-pressure gauge lead
4. Blue: usually the temperature gauge lead

The first two are Safe colors controlled by industry standards, though there are many other combinations unique to various manufacturers. If you work on a single brand of engine on a continuous basis, or if you're a vessel owner only concerned with his own engine, you may become very familiar with color patterns that apply to that engine.

But do not make any hard and fast assumptions if you address another engine. Wiring systems change, sometimes without notice, and occasionally they even change during a model year. The wire that you think goes to one appliance may be used for another.

Troubleshooting Gasoline Marine Engines - John Fleming

APPROACHING THE ENGINE

Assume you're able to read a wiring diagram, possess a volt/ohm meter (VOM), a soldering iron and a roll of low-temperature resin-core solder. Add to this an assortment of tinned wire terminals, a few colored lengths of heat-shrink tubing. Now we're ready to do battle.

Visual inspection will often tell which terminals are faulty. The VOM will read the circuits for the presence or absence of current and the presence or absence of continuity. The service manual will tell you where each is appropriate and the electrical values that you should read on the VOM.

If you suspect the plugs in the harness are faulty, you will find a diagram in the service manual that lays out both male and female plugs like a clock. The circuits which each pin or receptacle serves are designated.

HOW TO PROCEED

When you have determined that a terminal is faulty, it is simple to replace the offending part. If you have to replace short lengths of conductor, be certain you obtain the appropriate color and wire gauge. Solder all joints, and cover with heat-shrink tubing.

Crimp-on terminals are not acceptable for me, and short of a real emergency, there is no excuse good enough for their use. They not only fail frequently, but corrosion will create a resistance in them and they'll fry. This is very likely to create a terrible interference with your electronics, one for which you may hunt. And hunt.

PROBLEMS INSIDE THE HARNESS

Problems in the on-board wiring harness, other than the plug itself, can generally be cured by replacing the terminal or conductor. Terminals at the panel or switch also can be replaced. If the female plug is faulty, I replace the whole harness.

Internal problems within the panel harness are seldom repairable from outside the harness itself. This is not a terribly expensive item, and once the wiring problem has been isolated to the panel harness, I replace it. You may well save enough labor time that would have been spent cutting and splicing to pay for the thing.

WHAT IF THERE'S NO COLOR CODE?

Go to any good electrical shop and get a number pad. These have a set of numbered plastic strips with adhesive backing. You can wrap the terminal end of each conductor that you remove with a numbered strip. Then record the number and the purpose for which it was employed. Number pads have plenty of strips, and if you feel the need, you can wrap the conductor at both ends or in any other appropriate place which you deem necessary. Just be certain you have the same conductor each time you add a numbered strip. If you're about to overhaul an engine, or if for any reason you must remove the entire wiring harness, store it carefully in a clean, safe and dry place. Should those labels become lost, you will probably have a subsequent problem.

Replace the nuts on any appliance from which you remove a conductor. This will save a good deal of time in lost nuts or trying to identify the post on which a nut may belong.

Common sense is also useful in troubleshooting electrical problems. An example: Always check the battery voltage, both at the battery as well as at the point on the engine where current is delivered to the wiring harness. You can not read the proper voltage at the various terminals in the harness if the voltage is not available to the harness.

I once knew a mechanic who hunted low-voltage problems in the wiring harness for half a day before it occurred to him that the battery itself was low. (You simply can not get

Troubleshooting Gasoline Marine Engines - John Fleming

out more than you put in.)

Good wiring that you perform yourself should be protected from hot surfaces and abrasion. It should run in looms where indicated, pass through grommets at a bulkhead and generally enjoy the protection it deserves. Neat wiring is a beautiful thing to see, and you can be overly proud of quality work done in this area.

Troubleshooting Gasoline Marine Engines - John Fleming

CHAPTER TEN
THE ACCESSORIES

In general, manufacturers buy a basic engine from Chevrolet or Ford and then add certain accessories and sell it as a marine engine. This is called marinizing, but make no mistake: this is a true marine engine, not a car motor. A base engine is complete unto itself, assembled and sitting in a crate when shipped to the marinizer. Companies such as Mercury Marine, Crusader, Marine Power, even Volvo and Yamaha inboard or sterndrive, employ them.

There is a basic list of accessories that the marinizer adds. We will cover basic accessories in both this chapter and the next. Some marinizers like Mercury sell high-performance versions of their engines, and these may employ additional after-market parts you will not find in Chapters Ten and Eleven.

Superchargers, turbochargers, high-performance camshafts and related items come from other manufacturers, but for now let us consider the common accessories found on the stock engine. Accessories, like the engine they serve, are also made especially for marine applications, but they're made by various manufacturers. Some marinizers cast their own manifolds and elbows, but others use after-market parts. They differ greatly from automotive units in several ways. I'll list these accessories, then describe the general differences between the marine and the automotive. This chapter will confine itself to electrical and electronic accessories, plus the carburetor and fuel pump. The following chapter will concern

Troubleshooting Gasoline Marine Engines - John Fleming

itself with water-related items.
Consider the following:

1. Starter
2. Alternator
3. Carburetor
4. Fuel pump
5. Distributor

DIFFERENCES BETWEEN MARINE AND AUTOMOTIVE ACCESSORIES

Begin with the starter and alternator. These have a certain gauzing around the frame openings and are rated as totally enclosed and explosion-proof units, precluding the danger of fire in the bilge. Gasoline fumes are very explosive.

The carburetor has a flash arrestor atop the inlet and a suction port on the side. The suction port is attached to the fuel pump by a small-diameter hose which joins the fuel pump just atop the casting and withdraws any fuel that might spill off the top, should it rupture a diaphragm.

Fuel is drawn into the carburetor and drained into the intake manifold. This keeps the fuel out of the bilge or the crankcase. It saves the engine from dilution of lubricating oil and the bilge from a load of raw fuel. Neither of these features is found on automotive appliances.

The distributor has a gasket that lines the cap and seals the joint between. The purpose is to keep explosive fumes out of the distributor, a vital addition to an otherwise-deadly accessory.

WHAT ABOUT REPAIRS?

These are special items and thus deserve special care. Some we will fix ourselves, and some probably belong in a rebuild shop. The starter and alternator are two of the latter.

Troubleshooting Gasoline Marine Engines - John Fleming

Yes, given the proper equipment I can rebuild a starter or alternator and so can any competent mechanic, but should I? You can not match either the speed or the price with which a rebuilder produces them by the hundreds. If I use a rebuilt unit, I simply swap it across the counter. It has a guarantee, and I do not have the responsibility. Buy a rebuild.

HOW ABOUT THE CARBURETOR?

This is a toss-up. I build some carburetors and send some out. The reasons vary. The carburetor for a high-performance engine requires custom adjustments and jetting. I always rebuild these myself, and the information gathered from a spark plug insulator or a compression test often affects the adjustments.

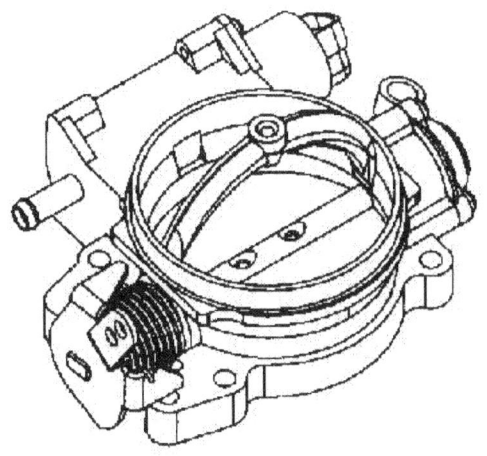

Figure 6
Courtesy of Mercury Marine

Top portion of the carburetor.

If you decide to rebuild the carburetor yourself, first buy the rebuild kit. Lay the exploded view out on a bench and disassemble the carburetor exactly as shown, placing the parts

Troubleshooting Gasoline Marine Engines - John Fleming

in a similar manner. Remove and discard all of the soft lead plugs from the carburetor body, plus each of the parts you intend to replace. Place their replacements into the scheme so that the entire group of pieces is once again a match for the exploded view. Place the carburetor body in a vat and soak it at least 24 hours.

Rinse off the carburetor body and blow all the passages clear with high-pressure air. Then reassemble the unit according to the exploded view. For a stock carburetor, the float-height adjustment specifications are shown in the same directions as the exploded view.

One advantage to be found in a factory-rebuilt carburetor is the use of a flow bench. Any reputable rebuilder flows and adjusts the carburetor before delivery. You should be able to install the rebuilt unit, and it will require little adjustment.

REBUILD THE DISTRIBUTOR?

Divide this question in two, those that apply to conventional distributors and those pertaining to electronic units.

Conventionals first. On a distributor with ignition points I'm willing to replace the points, condenser, rotor and distributor cap if needed. I'll occasionally replace the drive gear, but usually by the time the drive gear is sufficiently worn to need replacement, the bushings are worn out.

Now comes the question, which procedures should I perform myself and which should I send out? You can certainly replace and regap a set of ignition points. (Always replace; never try to sand or file a burned set of points unless there is a dire emergency.)

The job takes time, but the result is not very satisfactory, and it seldom lasts more than a very short while. What's worse, the mechanic's hourly charge while so engaged will just about pay for a new set of points anyway.

Replace the condenser (capacitor) every time you replace the points. The life of the points depends upon it. Be careful in greasing the rubbing block, and do not let grease contaminate the points themselves or they will quickly fail. If the distributor has a lubricator wick, be certain to properly adjust the space and angle of the wick. You can easily replace the rotor and distributor cap if needed.

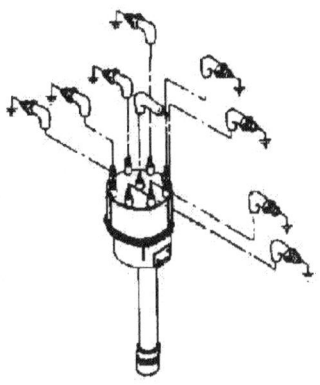

Figure 7
Courtesy of Mercury Marine

The typical distributor.

How about the drive gear? When the wear has reached the point where replacement is indicated, the distributor shaft bushings are generally worn out also. You can not adjust the points in a distributor with worn shaft bushings.

How do I recognize the problem? The simple way is to remove the rotor so that the points become visible. Take the distributor shaft in your hand and apply sideways pressure, back and forth. If the point gap changes to a visible degree, the bushings are gone. That movement will repeat itself while the engine is under way and the adjustment will suffer.

At this point I try to convince the owner to replace the conventional distributor and coil with an electronic unit. Generally I can make this replacement for just over $300. The

Troubleshooting Gasoline Marine Engines - John Fleming

savings in fuel, spark plugs, tune ups and other more general problems will quickly pay for the change.

Should I fail to make this sale, I'll buy a rebuilt conventional distributor. I have seen too many amateur efforts end in a bound distributor shaft and more money expended.

If the distributor is already an electronic unit in need of repair, I'll install a module, distributor cap or rotor when and if needed. Should you be required to install a module, be certain you set the air gap (the space between the module and the magnetic rotor) exactly according to the instructions. The module that fits your distributor generally has instructions for installation. If there are no instructions, consult the service manual. It is never a bad idea to do this anyway.

Most electronic distributors employ needle roller bearings on the shaft. They seldom need replacement, but if the electronic distributor does have needle roller bearings, I do not mind pressing these into the body, should they be required. They tend to self-align and if they're pressed in carefully, they will give no trouble.

If there is need to replace the drive gear on an electronic distributor, you're probably either using a high-performance camshaft, a high-pressure oil pump, or the camshaft may have too much end play. For high-performance units, you should change the distributor drive gear to one made of a stronger metal.

If the camshaft has too much end play, the thrust washer has probably failed and will need replacement. Failure to do this will result in early loss of the new drive gear and probably cause valve-train problems as well.

I'll deal with the camshaft and its problems during the chapters on overhaul. I do not know of any company that rebuilds electronic distributor bodies or distributors. These are fairly new anyway, and few have totally failed.

Approach the rebuilding or repair of any distributor carefully. This is not the most sophisticated machine on earth, but it is deserving of your care. It can play hob with your engine if you do not do your job.

CHAPTER ELEVEN
WATER-RELATED ACCESSORIES

Water related accessories have to do with cooling the engine and its parts. These accessories are often faced with the corrosion from the water that they circulate and the abrasion from the sand which wayward mariners sometimes feed to them. These are:

1. The circulating water pump
2. The raw water pump
3. The exhaust manifolds and elbows
4. The engine heat exchanger, if so equipped
5. The engine lubricating-oil heat exchanger
6. The transmission oil heat exchanger

WATER PUMPS

The circulating water pump employs a stainless-steel drive shaft, plus a saltwater-resistant impeller and seal. The raw water pump employs a stainless-steel drive shaft, a rubber impeller and a saltwater-resistant casing. The circulating water pump is different from an automotive unit, but of course the automotive engine does not employ a raw water pump.

I always buy a new or rebuilt circulating water pump if one should fail. These units are very low profit items to rebuild and not worth chasing the parts. It is another item where it would cost me more to build it myself than to buy from a rebuilder, and they generally do a very good job.

You may want to rebuild the raw water pump yourself. The pump manufacturer may offer a kit for this purpose, or you may have to buy each part separately. Always be sure to get all bearings, seals and the impeller, and also buy a cam. This is a bronze or stainless lump bolted inside the bottom of the housing. If this cam is badly worn and the pump housing has a similar problem, go ahead and get a new pump. I never rebuild marginal water pumps. To destroy an $8,000 engine for a $125 water pump is poor economy.

EXHAUST MANIFOLDS AND ELBOWS

Automotive engines do not require water-cooled manifolds or elbows, but they're a must on a marine engine. The heat from a straight-pipe exhaust would be totally unacceptable in a closed engine room. Besides being a fire hazard, the temperatures which result would be destructive to the vessel's structure.

The water-cooled exhaust manifold(s) and the elbow(s) on your engine are, in fact, water-jacketed exhaust pipes. Cooling water circulates around the exhaust passages and cools the system. The most drastic problems with these units are generally caused either by restriction or rust-through.

The possible causes for a total restriction are clogging from rust, salt or corrosion and dirt or sediment from shallow-water operation. This stops the flow of water and requires a total shut-down of the engine. Of course, an exhaust manifold can rust completely through. This usually occurs when a hole is blown in the exhaust port or passage, if you prefer that term. This allows hot gases to escape from the manifold, and surely this too requires immediate shut-down. There are less-drastic problems which rise with the exhaust manifold(s) and elbow(s) as well.

A more common problem with the exhaust system is leakage at the gaskets between manifold and elbow. This takes

Troubleshooting Gasoline Marine Engines - John Fleming

a bit longer, but in time it will ruin any engine. Evidence of this is seen as white streaks along the gasket edges between manifold and elbow, or rusty streaks down the sides of the casting, beginning at the joint. When you observe these conditions, replace the gaskets. I never use a sealer. The factory gaskets provided for this purpose are highly sophisticated in their design and will seal better and last longer without additional sealers.

Always check the machined sealing surfaces on the manifolds and elbows when you replace this gasket. The joints and any spacer plates must be very clean. Also check the thickness of the walls of the manifolds and the elbows. Machined surfaces should be at least 1/4" thick at the joint. Otherwise you should replace them. If the sealing surfaces are pitted or corroded, take them to the machine shop to be resurfaced. A milling machine will sometimes restore the seal at this joint.

Why is this manifold/elbow joint so very important? If it leaks to the outside of the engine, it almost surely leaks to the inside; directly into the cylinders the water goes. Valves, heads and perhaps an entire engine may be destroyed.

Other problems the exhaust manifolds and elbows encounter are clogging and corrosion. These can be caused by salt deposition, sand or silt from shallow water, or just plain rust scale. The culprit may be overheating of the engine. A raw water-cooled engine should run at 145_ Fahrenheit. Saltwater begins to desalinate and coat the block or manifolds at temperatures above this figure. Thus, the engine should be kept to this temperature.

This is not the most efficient temperature at which to operate the engine; you're dissipating too many BTUs of heat energy and wasting fuel. Yet there is no choice if the engine is to continue to operate. Keep your raw water-cooled engine at 145 degrees or less.

Troubleshooting Gasoline Marine Engines - John Fleming

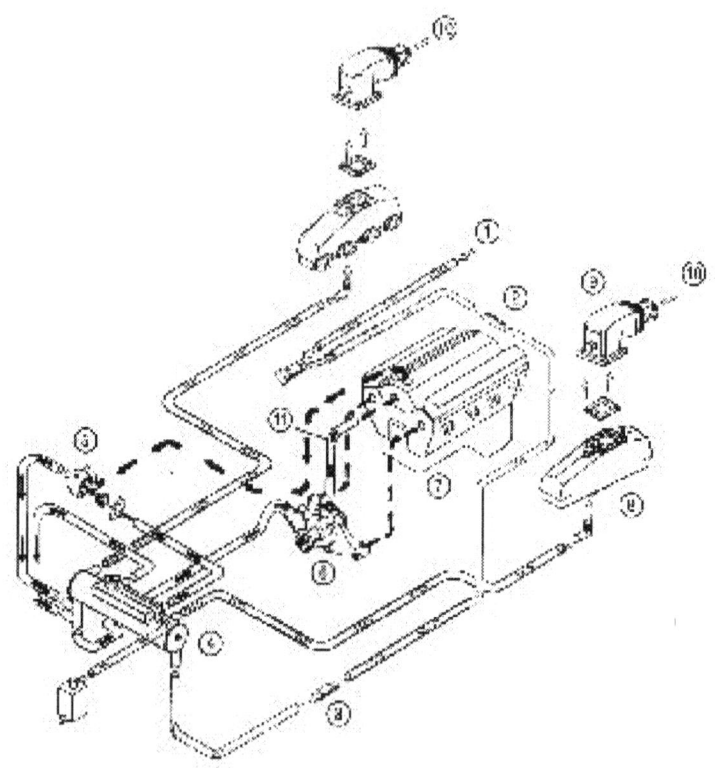

1- Seawater Intake (From Sterndrive)
2- Power Steering Cooler
3- Fuel Cooler, If Equipped
4- Heat Exchanger, Typical
5- Thermostat Housing and Cover Assembly
6- Engine Water Circulating Pump
7- Engine Block and Cylinder Head Assembly
8- Exhaust Manifold, Typical
9- Exhaust Elbow Assembly, Typical
10- Overboard (Water and Exhaust Discharge)
11- By-Pass Hose (454 and 502 CID Only)

Figure 8
Courtesy of Mercury Marine

Typical freshwater cooling system.

Troubleshooting Gasoline Marine Engines - John Fleming

THE ENGINE WITH FRESHWATER OR CLOSED-CIRCUIT COOLING

The heat exchanger is a cylindrical accessory about five inches in diameter and approximately 27" long. It sits atop or near the top of the engine, and it is distinguished by a filler cap that resembles a radiator cap on an automobile. Newer engines will have a clear-plastic coolant-recovery unit mounted in a lower location and attached by a small-diameter hose. This is generally made of plastic also. How does it work? The heat exchanger is no more than a water cooled radiator. Think of the radiator on your automobile with coolant in the coils and air flowing between those coils to remove heat from the coolant.

The heat exchanger on a boat uses sea water to cool the coils instead of air. Coolant from the engine circulates through the coils and sea water circulates around them. The sea water removes the heat from the coils and thence from the coolant.

What is the advantage? A freshwater-cooled engine generally runs at about 170_ Fahrenheit. There is no danger of the engine salting up since it has a closed circuit for its cooling and a coolant that will not corrode or solidify in the system.

Yet, the raw water that circulates inside the heat exchanger will desalinate and coat the heat exchanger itself if the temperature is excessive.

The 170_ figure is generally conceded to be about optimum. The engine cooled with a heat exchanger will dissipate fewer BTUs of heat energy than will a raw water-cooled engine but it still wastes a lot of fuel.

Troubleshooting Gasoline Marine Engines - John Fleming

POSSIBLE PROBLEMS WITH THE HEAT EXCHANGER

The most common problems are:
1. Overload
2. Leakage at the seals or gaskets
3. Internal leakage in the flues
4. Clogging or stoppage
5. The filler cap leaks
6. The zinc anode is depleted

In the order in which they're listed, consider the problems that normally assail the heat exchanger.

OVERLOAD

Some engines are equipped with an undersized heat exchanger, which is overworked from the start. This problem was manifest on a number of factory installations in the past. The engine created more BTUs of heat energy than the heat exchanger could dissipate or control. In this situation, the engine overheats from overload.

The manufacturer will usually come out with a replacement in a year or two, but as a mechanic you must approach this problem carefully. First, be certain there are no other problems causing the engine to overheat.

When you have isolated the problem to heat-exchanger overload, you will probably have to replace the heat exchanger with a larger model. There are sometimes alternatives, but they require substantial rearrangement of the cooling circuit.

Some engines include the exhaust manifolds in the freshwater cooling circuit. This is an excellent system since the manifolds are not exposed to saltwater. Yet a great deal of the heat exchanger's capacity is required to cool the manifolds. You can make alterations to the system and take the manifolds out of the freshwater circuit.

This is a drastic step, so you should be certain you know what you're doing. The cooling water will have to be rerouted, the block-off plates between manifold and elbow will need to be changed, and the hoses will have to be moved around. Unless you have done this before, do not attempt it alone, and then only as a last resort.

LEAKAGE AT SEALS OR GASKETS

The heat exchanger has a pair of end caps which are sealed or gasketed to close the ends. These end plates are removable for inspection and the seals sometimes leak. When they do so, replace them.

INTERNAL LEAKAGE

The heat exchanger may develop internal leaks. When this happens, there will be an exchange between the fresh water circuit and the raw water circuit. The coolant becomes contaminated and leaks out and the engine will surely overheat.

There is generally no repair for this problem. When the flues begin to go, I replace the heat exchanger.

If you suspect internal leakage have the unit pressure-tested. I use an ordinary radiator shop for this purpose.

BLOCKAGE

If the heat exchanger runs at excessive temperature for a long enough time, the inside may become salt coated or silted, and this will cause the engine to run even hotter. The salt or silt residue can generally be flushed or otherwise removed from the system. I use an ordinary radiator shop for this purpose.

Troubleshooting Gasoline Marine Engines - John Fleming

THE FILLER CAP LEAKS

The filler cap on a heat exchanger is a pressure cap, just like the one on your automobile. It has a value embossed on it. If the unit leaks, it may simply be worn out and ready for replacement. If the cap tests OK but the leakage continues, you may have internal problems with the engine.
Remove the cap and run the engine. Do you see bubbles forming in the heat exchanger? Coupled with a poor compression reading, this is another indication that a head gasket may be blown or some other internal problem.

THE ZINC ANODE IS DEPLETED

When the zinc anode is 25 percent depleted, its effectiveness is 100-percent gone. This pencil-shaped part is screwed in the side of the heat exchanger body with a brass, six-side head exposed to view. Replace it often, for this is the life of your heat exchanger.

THE OIL HEAT EXCHANGERS

I'll address these parts simultaneously since they're constructed alike and have similar problems. They're generally located in the raw-water intake hose, and they're the first accessories exposed to the cool incoming water. Each is attached to the engine or transmission that it serves with a delivery hose and a return hose.
Lube oil and transmission oil heat exchangers are designed to keep the oil temperature within tolerances. They operate in the same manner as the engine heat exchanger, but they have oil on one side of the circuit instead of coolant.
The raw water circulates around the flues and cools the oil inside. This is a good system and provides a needed function, but these are dangerous parts and they should be watched carefully. What are the potential problems? A pin hole

Troubleshooting Gasoline Marine Engines - John Fleming

in either of these units can leak all of the lubricant out into the cooling water and thence overboard! If you're losing lube oil or transmission oil and you can not discover where it is going, consider a pressure test on the oil heat exchanger. Water in the crankcase or transmission oil will reinforce this possibility.

These heat exchangers will also clog from seaweed. If the vessel is not equipped with a raw-water intake strainer (they all should be but many are not), seaweed or other incoming material can pile up against the flues of the oil heat exchanger. Remember. this is the first accessory that the incoming raw water meets. This blockage will close off or impair the flow of coolant with potentially drastic results.

Water and coolant flow are a large part of the life of the engine, and problems with these accessories are often misunderstood, one problem being mistaken for another. Consider this chapter carefully. Get yourself a cooling-circuit diagram and study it as well. One day you will be glad that you did.

Troubleshooting Gasoline Marine Engines - John Fleming

CHAPTER TWELVE
DISASSEMBLY & INSPECTION OF THE CYLINDER HEADS

Disassembly of the engine and inspection of the parts proceeds in essentially the same manner, regardless of whether the engine is conventional or electronic. There are many ways in which to disassemble the engine, and you may have a preference of your own.

This chapter will be confined to disassembly and inspection of the cylinder heads and the parts or accessories attached thereto. However, the procedure for cylinder-head removal is the same as that for removing the engine from the boat up to a certain point. I'll mark that point and not repeat the procedure when we begin to remove an engine.

UNIVERSAL STEPS FOR REMOVAL OF CYLINDER HEADS OR COMPLETE ENGINES

1. Before you begin any disassembly, obtain two things: plastic zip-lock bags; pints, quarts, and gallons will be sufficient. The second item will be a book of numbered plastic adhesive-backed strips. Electric shops carry these. What are

Troubleshooting Gasoline Marine Engines - John Fleming

they for? With a few exceptions, you will place all of the nuts and bolts that you remove in these bags, keeping them segregated to the assembly or accessory from which they were taken.

Use a masking-tape strip and a marker to label each bag. This will save an unbelievable amount of time during reassembly. Why not bag up all of the nuts and bolts? You may wish to replace some onto or into the place from which they came. Fastenings in this category are usually employed on electrical terminals, control cables, etc. Any bolt or washer not attached directly to such a spot goes into a bag. Nuts, bolts and washers from all the major assemblies such as intake manifold bolts, cylinder head bolts, rocker cover bolts and similar parts each goes into its own bag with a label. Other bolts should be handled in like manner. You can not believe how much sorting and picking this will save.

What are the numbered adhesive-backed, tape strips for? The wiring harness will be color-coded if you have a factory part, and you should be able to get any information you need about that harness from the wiring diagram in the service manual. Yet, I never take a chance. I wrap a tape strip around each conductor in the wiring harness. In fact, I label every conductor that is attached to the engine and record the number along with the purpose of the conductor on the electrical notebook. This can be helpful with any engine, but it is absolutely essential if the engine has been rewired without the benefit of a color code.

2. Label all conductors to be removed from their terminals. The coil lead, tach wire, temperature gauge and oil-pressure sending unit are generally on top of the engine. There may be others, so check carefully. Label each and record the numbers. Now shut off all power to the engine and disconnect the battery leads, then remove the necessary conductors and wrap the harness out of the way. We did this first because removal of the fuel system parts may drain at least some fuel into the bilge, and we want to be free of any chance of making a spark.

Troubleshooting Gasoline Marine Engines - John Fleming

3. Before removing any parts of the engine, shut the fuel lines off at the tank and then remove the fuel line from the carburetor inlet. Keep a good supply of rags on hand and wipe up all spillage. Now drain the fuel line into a proper container and clean up any residue. Place the fuel line in an out-of-the-way position out of the bilge so that water can not enter the line.

4. Drain the block and the exhaust manifolds. Drain the coolant from the heat exchanger if one is provided. If the engine is coming out of the boat, I drain the oil at this point. Otherwise, I leave the oil in the crankcase until the valve job is completed, then drain and replace the oil before restarting the engine.

In either case, I like to draw an oil sample for analysis before I remove the cylinder heads if the owner will agree. This oil sample, when analyzed by a good laboratory, will give a very good picture of the condition of the rest of the engine. It will also help you to determine if further tear-down is indicated or if a simple valve-grind job is sufficient.

5. Using a numbered plastic tape strip, identify the throttle and shift cables. Remove the cables from the engine and identify the attachment bolts or nuts as you wish. Coil the cables and store out of the way.

6. Remove the connectors that attach the exhaust manifolds to the exhaust hoses. I have a group of tapered wooden plugs which I turned on a lathe that fit the various sized hoses very well. I put one of these plugs in each hose end and place a single clamp on it. Some people use PVC fittings or other plugs for this purpose, but you should have some kind of plug, regardless of what you elect to use. Hang the pipes or hoses as high up in the engine room as you can get them and support them there. Those hoses or pipes open directly to the sea, and a careless hand here can sink a ship.

7. Close off the raw-water intake cocks, then remove all hoses from the engine, including those from the heat exchanger. I use a wooden plug and clamp in this line.

8. Remove the wiring harness, using numbered plastic

Troubleshooting Gasoline Marine Engines - John Fleming

tape strips to identify each conductor.

NOTE: THE REMAINING INSTRUCTIONS ARE TO BE FOLLOWED FOR CYLINDER HEAD REMOVAL ONLY.

9. Remove electrical or other accessories mounted on the cylinder head. This includes the ignition coil. Remember to bag and label the bolts.

10. Remove the carburetor if one is involved and bag the bolts. If the engine has EFI, remove the injectors and the injector wiring harness. Remove any seals or gaskets between the injectors and the manifold. Remove the fuel rail and any fittings.

11. Detach the plug wires at the spark plug end and remove the distributor.

12. Remove the spark plugs.

13. Remove the intake manifold and bag the bolts.

14. Remove any accessories such as fuel or oil filters connected to the exhaust manifolds. Remove the fuel lines or oil lines to these accessories, if present. Now remove the exhaust manifold and bag the bolts from the manifolds and each of these accessories.

15. Remove the rocker covers. This may seem a bit out of place, but it will readily become apparent that on many engines these covers have outside bolts next to the exhaust manifold which can not be removed until the exhaust manifolds are gone. Remember to bag the bolts.

16. Release the rocker-arm adjustment nuts, then remove the rocker arms, push rods and rocker-arm pivot balls. You can also remove the cam followers (lifters). I keep the entire group of parts, including the lifter, in a single bag. During reassembly I replace each part into the position from which it came unless, it proves to be faulty and needs replacement.

17. Remove the cylinder-head bolts, releasing them in the same sequence in which they were originally installed. Release the pressure in three measured increments of about 35 pounds each. Consult the service manual for the proper

tighten/release sequence. Bag the bolts.
18. Remove the cylinder head.
19. Clean up! There will be some residue to enter the cylinders, water, coolant, etc., so remove this material. Then thoroughly oil the cylinder walls and the block deck. Cover the top of the engine with a clean cloth. Oil the sealing surfaces on the cylinder head.

TAKE THE HEAD AND EXHAUST MANIFOLD TO A GOOD MACHINE SHOP

It is time now to buy your gasket set, which will contain the valve stem seals that the machine shop needs and you can deliver at this time. You may not or may not be satisfied with the seals furnished in this kit. If they're not suitable to your needs, buy a set.

1. Have the valve stems checked for diameter. Have the valve guides checked for diameter. (The machinist will have the maximum allowable clearance figures, dependent upon the particular engine). Have the valve springs and any dampers checked on the tensiometer.
Check the cylinder head sealing surfaces for straightness (.002 thousandths maximum). This should include the block side of the head and the ports at the exhaust manifold connections. Also test the exhaust manifold at the port outlets. Check any and all freeze plugs on the cylinder heads and manifolds.
2. Test the head and valve seats for cracks or leaks. Use a die test or similar. Have the valve seats reground, and if they're too deeply sunken into the cylinder heads, have hard (stellite or comparable) seats installed.
3. Regrind the valve faces, and check for thickness of the valve heads after grinding. If the valve head is not at least .060 thousandths thick after the grind, replace it. A valve with a sharp edge will glow and cause detonation, just as extended

Troubleshooting Gasoline Marine Engines - John Fleming

threads on the spark plug will. A sharp-edged valve will fail at an early time.

4. Have the rocker studs checked for height, and if any show the slightest indication of being above the proper height, either have them pinned or obtain screw-in studs.

5. Have the machine shop reassemble the cylinder heads (I prefer heavy-duty Teflon valve stem seals). Then recheck the valve-spring tension with the entire assembly in place atop the head.

Do not automatically assume that the machine shop will do each of these things. They may routinely do so, and we will be pleased if this is true, but do not be afraid to designate the things you want done. Listen carefully to the machinist, and if he has additional suggestions, you or the owner of the vessel should carefully consider them.

By the time the machine shop is work is completed, you should have the results of your oil analysis and know if you're ready to reassemble the engine.

REASSEMBLY

Before you begin reassembly, you should take all those bolts and run the threads through a wire-wheel buffer. Clean and lightly oil the threads. Now run a die through the threaded holes in the heads or block. Clean them thoroughly and oil them lightly. You should now get a good torque reading.

As you buff the exhaust manifold bolts or others exposed to corrosion, check the heads for straightness, the bodies for rust or corrosion, and the threads for condition. Replace any bolt that looks even slightly questionable.

Replace each part in the reverse order from that in which it was removed. Use the torque values and sequence provided in the service manual. The numbers and procedure will vary for each make and model.

Troubleshooting Gasoline Marine Engines - John Fleming

A FEW SUGGESTIONS

Coat the base of the lifters with camshaft break-in lube and return them to their original holes. Coat the rocker-arm mounting balls with STP or a similar lubricant. Coat the tips of the push rods with camshaft break-in lube. Coat the valve stems with oil.

Be very careful when installing the intake manifold gasket; a leak here is a real problem. Be certain you have the cylinder head gaskets turned in the proper direction atop the block before installing the head. Be careful when lowering the cylinder head onto the gasket. If you mark the gasket, it will leak.

Install the distributor and the plug wires. Do not install the spark plugs at this time.

Install the fuel injectors exactly according to the instructions in the service manual. They're easily damaged.

Remember those rocker covers? Install them now, or you may not be able to do so after the exhaust manifolds are in place. Take care with the rocker cover gaskets, and tighten the mounting bolts in sequence.

Replace the exhaust manifolds and elbows. Torque the bolts according to the instructions in the service manual, and do not use any type of sealer on the gaskets between the cylinder head and exhaust manifold. Wait until you have the exhaust manifolds in place before installing a new set of spark plugs. They're easily broken during installation of the exhaust manifold. Now attach the plug wires in the proper sequence according to the firing order for the particular engine.

Replace the heat exchanger if the engine was so equipped. Replace all drain plugs and the zinc pencil anode. Replace the hoses and the coolant, then reattach the coolant recovery unit.

Reattach the fuel and oil filter bodies to the appropriate mounting spot on the engine, whether this is the exhaust manifold or other location. Be certain that any plugs are out of the water lines or exhaust hoses before hook-up, then reconnect the water and the fuel lines and the control cables.

I save the on-board wiring harness for a near-the-last job so that I'll not bruise the conductors as I move heavy parts around. After it is installed, open the appropriate fuel and water valves, then replace the 12-volt power supply to the engine.

CHANGE THE OIL AND FILTER

When the job is finished and the last danger of oil contamination is past, replace the dirty oil and oil filter cartridge before start-up. Take a good look around. Your assigned task was a valve job, but you should look for any other problems that might cause that job to fail.

CHAPTER THIRTEEN
BEFORE YOU DISASSEMBLE THE ENGINE

There is a great deal of misunderstanding about engine rotation. I may be about to muddy the water a bit, but I'll try to explain the elements of engine rotation as they apply to marine engines because this is critical. The designation for a marine engine is not the same as that for an automobile, and the potential for disaster are many.

The engine is no more than a pump. It pumps air into the carburetor and out the exhaust. If you put the wrong starter on the engine, it will turn backwards. Then it will pump water into the engine and out the carburetor. You must get the rotation right.

Here are some hints:

PORT SIDE

1. Look at the engine from the propeller end. Almost all modern marine engines drive from the flywheel end of the engine; thus the flywheel is the drive or propeller end, and it is from here that the direction of rotation is measured. For the next few paragraphs, assume we're talking about an engine that drives from the flywheel end. The left-hand engine mounts on the port side of the boat and turns outboard, or counter-clockwise when viewed from the propeller, and it turns a left-

hand propeller. The serial number for this engine may include an "L" for Left, an "N" for Normal, or an "S" for Standard rotation. Although this engine may turn the same way as an automobile, in marine parlance it is a left-hand engine.

2. Again, looking at the engine from the flywheel or propeller end, the right-hand engine mounts on the starboard side of the boat and turns outboard, or in this case, clockwise. The serial number may contain an "R" for right hand, a "C" for counter- rotating, or an "O" for opposite rotation. Although this engine turns in the opposite direction from an automobile, it is still designated as right-hand in marine terminology.

IF THE ENGINE DRIVES FROM THE TIMING-GEAR END

The same rules apply. Engine rotation is measured from the propeller-end of the boat, and there is a great deal of misunderstandings about this.

The manufacturer or parts house will be much more likely to give you the correct part if you provide a serial number rather than trying to tell in what direction the engine rotates. When the serial number is missing from the engine, what's your best move? Turn the engine over with the starter before removing it from the boat, and mark the direction of rotation on each part. Draw the direction of rotation of both engine and starter on a piece of paper in such a manner as to have no confusion.

How about the similarities and the differences in the internal parts of standard- and opposite-rotation engines. In modern engines, the starters turn in opposite directions, the camshafts turn in the same direction, and the water pump and distributor turn in the same direction.

The standard-rotation engine turns left hand, viewed from the flywheel. The camshaft is driven with a timing chain, and it turns left-hand also. A gear on the camshaft drives the distributor and oil pump. The opposite-rotation engine turns right hand, viewed from the flywheel. However, the camshaft is driven with two direct meshing gears instead of a chain.

The gear drives the camshaft in the opposite direction from the crankshaft or left-hand rotation. Now the camshaft, the oil pump and the distributor all turn the same way on both engines. However, there is a substantial difference in the firing order.

How do you deal with this? Use the engine serial number and the service manual to determine direction of rotation, firing order- and cylinder-numbering sequence (this according to the manufacturer). If you have a proper serial number, use the manufacturer's directions exclusively. If not, you will need a very good mechanic indeed.

A SIMPLE CHART

LEFT-HAND

1. Turns left hand propeller.
2. Has "L", "S", or "N" in serial number.
3. Drives camshaft with chain.
4. Same direction as the engine turns.
5. Firing sequence same as auto.
6. Cylinders are numbered same as auto.
7. The distributor turns clockwise.

RIGHT-HAND ENGINE

1. Turns right hand propeller.
2. Has "R", "O", or "C" in serial number.
3. Drives camshaft with a gear.
4. Opposite to the way engine turns.
5. Firing sequence different from auto.
6. Cylinders are numbered same as auto.
7. The distributor turns clockwise.

Although the camshafts turn in the same direction,

they're not ground the same. The lobes are arranged for a different firing order.

AN EXAMPLE USING A CHEVROLET SMALL-BLOCK, BOTH ENGINES

From the timing-gear end of the engine: The cylinders number 1-3-5-7 on the right side and 2-4-6-8- on the left. This is true of both engines. The firing sequence on the left hand-rotation engine (the same as an automobile) is 1-8-4-3-6-5-7-2. The firing order on the right hand-rotation Engine (opposite rotation to the automobile) is 1-2-7-5-6-3-4-8.

A FIRING SEQUENCE APPEARS ON THE INTAKE MANIFOLD

Not a reliable source, I'm sorry to say. The intake manifolds are the same as on an automobile, and all engines that rotate in either direction have the same intake manifolds with the same firing sequence embossed upon their surface. This has caused no small amount of anxiety in past times. No service manual I have ever seen warned of this potential problem.

ANTIQUE ENGINES

When you begin to repair or restore older engines, you will quickly realize they have at times been driven from either end of the engine and that the designations of rotation or the firing order will reflect this diversity. I heartily recommend you mark everything on all engines, but especially on the antiques prior to tear-down.

Chris-Craft and other companies once made what some purists call "true opposite-rotation engines." These drove the camshaft with a timing gear on both engines. The camshafts

Troubleshooting Gasoline Marine Engines - John Fleming

rotated in opposite directions, the oil pumps rotated in opposite directions, the distributors rotated in opposite directions and the whole business was a nightmare. These engines also drove from the timing-gear end, and all bets were off when determining direction of rotation. Some enterprising mechanics even converted some of these engines to drive off the flywheel! Unless very good records appeared in the ship's log, no one knew what was going on.

Any time that you change engines or do any major work to an engine, you should record the work, including all pertinent details in the ship's log.

NEW ENGINES

Most modern engines all turn in the same direction. No opposite-rotation engines have been manufactured by Chevrolet since 1998 because the transmission changes the direction of rotation between shafts and propellers. The propellers still turn in opposite directions, left hand on the port side and right hand on the starboard, yet the engines rotate in the same direction.

If I have done nothing else, I hope I have at least emphasized that you monitor engine rotation before making any major tear-down. Some fine mechanics never quite seem to get this matter of numbers and firing sequence straight in their minds. But if they're successful, they all recognize the fact that they must make accommodation.

Get your numbers right, then tear the engine down.

Troubleshooting Gasoline Marine Engines - John Fleming

CHAPTER FOURTEEN
COMPLETE ENGINE DISASSEMBLY

In Chapter Twelve we broke the engine down to the block by removing the carburetor, the intake manifold, all the accessories attached to the heads and the cylinder heads themselves. We did this in a systematic manner and pursued the exercise on the assumption that we'd look at all procedures short of a complete engine tear-down.

We approach this chapter on the assumption that the engine must be completely disassembled. Naturally, we will not do this inside the vessel; removal of the engine is required. The first order of business is to determine the direction of rotation for the engine.

If no serial number can be found, turn the engine over with the starter and carefully mark the direction of rotation for both the engine and the starter. If you're about to disassemble a twin-engine pair, be certain you keep the parts isolated and good markings for each. Record all drawings, numbers and engine marks on a notebook.

Now go back to Chapter Twelve and borrow a few procedures. Begin with the baggies and obtain a book of numbered and gummed plastic strips. You already know what these are for.

Be certain that the lifting chains or cables are sufficiently strong to lift the engine with a very large safety factor. Before the engine enters the shop I drain the crankcase

Troubleshooting Gasoline Marine Engines - John Fleming

oil and engine coolant (freshwater cooling) into proper containers.

When you have the engine in the shop, disconnect and remove the transmission. Remove any accessories such as the oil filter body that may be mounted on the exhaust manifolds or cylinder heads, then remove the exhaust manifolds and elbows. Bag and label all the nuts and bolts.

Remove the bell housing, drive plate and flywheel. Bag and label the nuts and bolts. If the engine has an external sealing system at the rear main, remove the seal housings and the rear main seal. Now you may lift the engine and attach it to the engine stand.

If you're building both engines from a twin-screw installation, I always set those engines on opposite sides of the shop. Using the front shop door as the bow of the boat, I place them to port and starboard just as they came from the vessel. I keep the parts separate at all times, and I never go back and forth, working first on one engine then the other. Whatever you do, do not give yourself an opportunity to mix parts or confuse specifications.

Remove the carburetor or injector system, the distributor, the intake manifold and the cylinder heads in the same manner as in Chapter Thirteen. Remove the block-mounted accessories, the starter, alternator. raw-water pump and the circulating water pump. Bag and label all the nuts and bolts.

Now you're ready to begin disassembling the cylinder block. Remove the crankcase pan and then the timing cover in that order. The pan seals against the lower side of the timing cover, and the timing cover must be removed first or damage will result to the sheet metal.

Remove the oil pump and pickup screen. Remove the timing chain/gear/ and the camshaft. Be very careful with the camshaft. You should learn to remove and replace one of these without scarring or scratching the cam shaft bearings. This is a delicate job, and I always perform it with the timing gear still bolted to the camshaft.

Troubleshooting Gasoline Marine Engines - John Fleming

I lay the engine stand on its spindle-end with the engine block sticking upward. I can then use the timing gear to better control the movement of the cam shaft and lift it straight up. I always replace cam shaft (timing) gears and or chains. If a cam bearing is not worn, I let it remain as it is.

Raise the engine stand back onto the wheels and remove the timing gear from the crankshaft; you will need a proper puller. (This part is installed with a tight fit.) With the engine upright on the stand, inspect the cylinders for a ridge. Almost any engine will have some ridge at the top of the bore after many hours of operation. Using a ridge reamer, remove the cylinder ridge from the bores. You may want to get some help with at least the first one or two of these. The reamer will remove too much material from the cylinders if it is improperly handled. Try to get all of the ridge, but no more. The reason for this is twofold. While an old and experienced mechanic can usually look at a cylinder and tell if it will need boring, you should try to save the pistons, the piston rings, and the connecting rods, just in case.

The pistons will not come out of the bores easily if that ridge is there. The connecting rods are going to bear the brunt of your efforts to remove the assembly. So for the sake of an orderly disassembly procedure, you must remove the ridge from the bores, then put two tablespoons of lubricating oil in each cylinder.

Look carefully at the big ends of the connecting rods. Are they marked and numbered? The numbers indicate the cylinder on which they belong. The markings indicate which way the rod cap sits on the rod when it is properly matched.

There may be only numbers on both halves of the connecting rod. In that case, you will know that the numbered sides of the rod and cap are a match. If you see a pair of numbers, one up and one down when you assemble the rod and cap together, you have them correctly aligned.

Before you start to remove the connecting rods, cut two pieces of rubber hose of a diameter that will fit tightly on the rod bolts. Cut the hose into pieces about six inches long.

Troubleshooting Gasoline Marine Engines - John Fleming

When you finish with this, save the hoses; you will use them to reassemble the engine

If the rods and caps are already properly marked, you may begin to remove them. If not, mark them well. Using a set of stencils, stamp the rod and cap with the number of the cylinder in which they appear. Then start their removal.

Remove both nuts and any locks from a single rod. Keep the bolts, locks, rod cap and insert bearings from each rod in a separate container. Do not mix them up. Remove the caps very carefully, being certain that the rod bolts do not come in contact with the crankshaft.

Slip the rubber tubes on the rod bolts to protect the shaft as you remove the piston/rod assembly. Use the wooden handle of a hammer or a one-inch wooden dowel to push the assembly out the top of the cylinder. Be prepared to catch the piston as it emerges form the bore. If the assembly is reluctant to emerge, tap lightly on the connecting rod. Please, please be careful. I use a light hammer and a one inch dowel between the rod and the hammer. If you have removed the ridge properly and lightly oiled the bores, the assembly should come easily. Remove all the piston and rod assemblies.

Next, turn the engine upside down on the stand and inspect the main bearing caps. Be certain the caps are numbered, and if they're not, get out the stencil again. When you're quite certain that you can restore the main bearing caps to the same spot on the block from which they emerged, you're ready to remove the crankshaft. All the nuts and bolts should be bagged and labeled.

Place each main bearing cap with its bearings and nuts and bolts in a separate bag. When all of these bearing caps are removed, you may pick up the crankshaft. After it is out of the engine, stand it on its end with a soft piece of wood underneath the flange. Use a corner or safe place in the shop. Never, ever store a crankshaft or camshaft flat on any surface.

Your disassembly is complete, but you still have a number of things to do before you go to the machine shop. Many mechanics send off an engine before it is ready to go.

Troubleshooting Gasoline Marine Engines - John Fleming

The result is not very satisfactory, and the mechanic can blame no one but himself.

In the next chapter we will discuss all the things that must be done to prepare the engine for reassembly. Every one is important, and none will bear ignoring.

Attention to detail is important during disassembly. During this process we sought to insure that no part of the engine be damaged, that we become familiar with the location of each part, that no part be lost, and that each nut or bolt be properly identified.

For preparation and reassembly that attention to detail is even more important.

Troubleshooting Gasoline Marine Engines - John Fleming

CHAPTER FIFTEEN
PREPARING THE ENGINE FOR MACHINE WORK

Before you take your engine to the machine shop, remove all freeze plugs from every hole in the block. Brass plugs are sold in kits, and you should buy one. The inner water passages in the block can not be cleaned completely if these plugs are not removed.

Remove the screwed-in plugs with square heads at the ends of the cylinder block. These seal the ends of the oil-galley passages and these carry oil to the vital parts of the engine. Many mechanics do not do this, relying on the vatting process at the machine shop as a sole source of cleaning. This is not a satisfactory method.

When you have removed all the plugs out of both ends of the block, take a rifle ramrod with a wire brush and run it through and through the gallery holes. Use plenty of solvent and lots of high-pressure air. When the solvent comes out clean and clear, you're ready for the machine shop.

THE MACHINING PROCESS

Your machinist will generally make all of the necessary checks to see if the engine parts are or are not within allowable tolerances. Give him plenty of room, but know which things are to be checked, how they're to be checked, and if indeed

Troubleshooting Gasoline Marine Engines - John Fleming

each of those things is checked.

Below is are the parts which should be checked for tolerances:

1. Cylinder block
2. Crankshaft
3. Connecting rods
4. Pistons
5. Camshaft
6. Cylinder heads
7. Valve seats
8. Valves
9. Rocker arms
10. Rocker studs
12. Rocker-arm mounting balls
13. Push rods
14. Valve springs/dampers
15. Valve-spring retainers/stem locks

NORMAL CHECKS FOR EACH PART

Check the engine block for a straight and flat deck (top). It should be flat, within a maximum allowable error of .002". If it does not satisfy this requirement, deck the block.

Check the cylinder bores for diameter. They should be within .004" of the original factory specification, with no more than .002" taper. If this specification is not met, bore the block, but as little as possible. You will not realize any more power with a .060" overbore than you will with a .020" overbore. You might want to rebuild the engine again some day, so leave yourself a bit of room.

Bore the block to within about .001" to .0005" of finish specification, and finish up with a hone. You should have a light crosshatch pattern visible on the walls of the cylinders. When you're through with the top of the block, it is time for the bottom. Check the alignment of the main bearings; there should be no more than .001" misalignment between the bearings. If the block can not satisfy this requirement, align-bore the block. In order to make this effective, it will be necessary to first mill a few thousandths of an inch off the main caps. Then do the align-boring procedure. If the engine has ever spun a main-bearing insert in the past, the block should be align-bored regardless of the measurements.

It is wise to remember that insert bearing shells are not round. They're oblong, and they crush, becoming perfectly round as the caps are tightened. This crush applies strong pressure to the bearing shells and helps to hold them in place. If a main bearing insert has previously spun inside one of the mains, it is more likely to do so again. Go ahead and align-bore the block.

As a last operation, have the block vatted.

THE CRANKSHAFT

Your machinist will check the crankshaft and advise you of needed repairs. Do not automatically assume any dimension or procedure for the crankshaft. If you can polish out the scratches and go back with a standard dimension bearing, do so. If you can turn the crankshaft to only a .001" or .002" bearing, do this.

A machine shop that routinely turns everything to one or two standard dimensions is robbing you of the potential to build the engine several times. Turn the crankshaft as needed and no more.

OVERSIZE PISTONS

When you have the block bored, you will need a set of oversize pistons. Buy them before you bore the block. If you're using original-equipment pistons, have the machine shop bore the block to the exact clearance recommended in the service manual. If you're using after-market pistons, ignore the service

Troubleshooting Gasoline Marine Engines - John Fleming

manual and have them fit according to the manufacturer's recommendation. You decide whether you want after-market parts, but whichever part you select, install them according to the manufacturer's wishes.

Oversize pistons require a matching set of oversize rings. I buy rings that are pre-fit. There is really no reason to file a set of rings for a custom gap unless you're fitting up a racing engine. Have the machine shop install the pistons on the connecting rods unless or until you're familiar with this procedure.

CONNECTING RODS

Connecting rods should be tested for diameter and roundness at both the little and big ends. If they're in specification, they should be further tested on a go/no-go gauge. This establishes the presence or lack of any twist. If the connecting rods are not exactly on the factory specifications, rebuild them.

CAMSHAFT

The camshaft should be checked with a micrometer for wear at the lobes and the journals. The camshaft journals are oiled directly from the gallery, and any excessive wear in the bearings or the journals can lead to low oil pressure from the beginning. Irregular lobes on the camshaft will lead to very poor performance. Be certain that the camshaft and cam bearings are within proper specifications or replace them. If the engine has more than 1,000 hours operating time, it will almost surely require the replacement of both bearings and camshaft.

CYLINDER HEADS

These should be die-tested or magnafluxed for cracks in the head or valve seats. The heads should be checked for straightness. No more than a .002" feeler gauge should go between a Starret straight edge and the head surface. The exhaust-port faces between the cylinder head and the exhaust manifolds should be checked in a similar fashion.

Valve guides should be checked for diameter and new guides inserted if necessary. I like heavy-duty Teflon valve-stem seals. You may have to broach the guide stems for these, and if this is to be done, now is the time to do so.

Do all guide and surface work before attempting to grind the valve seats. I prefer a three-angle grind. When the seats are ground, slip the valves into the holes one at a time. If any valve is recessed too far into the head, you should have a hard seat installed.

Valves seats that are ground down into the head cause a loss of breathing to the engine and a consequent loss of power. This is a common flaw in the work of many machine shops. The customer is often told, "I had to take off that much metal to get a good seat." This may be true, but the result is still not acceptable. Go ahead and install a hard seat.

VALVES

Valves stems should be measured for diameter before grinding. If they're worn, there is no reason to grind them. Replace all valves with excessive stem wear. Now grind all of the old valves and check the thickness of the head. Any valve that does not have a proper thickness on the side should be discarded and replaced.

Why not measure the thickness before grinding? The grinder will remove some metal from the head, and we need to consider the thickness after this metal has been removed.

ROCKER ARMS, ROCKER BALLS AND ROCKER STUDS

Rocker arms should be inspected at the wear points for

scars or scratches. The mounting balls should receive a similar treatment. The rocker arm mounting studs should be inspected for height if they're pressed into the cylinder-head bosses. Loose studs should be replaced and pinned. If the studs are the screw-in variety, they need only be checked for thread tension (torquing). During a valve job I always remove screw-in studs, clean the threads in head and block, then reinstall. (Use Lock-Tite on the threads and torque to factory specs.)

VALVE SPRINGS AND DAMPERS

These should be tested for tension at the proper installed height. Spring retainers and stem locks should be inspected for burrs or chipped pieces. Look at every one of them. It is usually preferable to allow the machine shop to assemble the cylinder heads. The job is not costly, and they can usually do this more rapidly than you or I.

If this is a custom, high-performance engine or if you simply believe that you will do a better job, you may wish to assemble your own heads. This is not a process that will tax the talents of an Einstein, but it is important that it be done properly. Anyone undertaking the task should get a bit of help on the first attempt.

While the parts to be machined are at the shop, you can clean the tin parts from the engine. Carefully inspect all the sheet-metal parts such as the timing cover, rocker covers and the crankcase pan. Replace any that are thin or heavily rusted. Clean all gasket surfaces, and be certain that no portion of the old gasket remains.

Check the accessories. The starter, alternator, distributor and water pumps should be inspected, tested and repaired or replaced as needed. Pressure-test the heat exchanger and the exhaust manifolds, along with the engine-oil and clutch-oil heat exchangers. If you do this now, you will be ready to go when the machine shop returns the remachined parts.

Troubleshooting Gasoline Marine Engines - John Fleming

When the machine shop is finished, bring the parts back to your shop. Run a tap through the bolt holes and wire-brush the threads on all bolts. Replace any that are worn. Lightly oil the threads. Do the whole thing, including the rifle brush in the block passages.

Clean each part of the engine completely. When this is done, lay out everything on the bench in the order in which it is to be installed. You're now ready to reassemble the engine.

Troubleshooting Gasoline Marine Engines - John Fleming

CHAPTER SIXTEEN
REASSEMBLE THE ENGINE

If you have bet on the ball game or your wife burned the toast, wait until tomorrow. There are several hundred parts in any engine, which means that there are several hundred opportunities to make an error during reassembly.

Concentrate.

LUBRICATE THE CAMSHAFT BEARINGS

Before you do anything, lubricate the camshaft bearings. Turn the engine upside down on the engine stand. Reach inside the cylinder block, working from the bottom, and generously coat the camshaft bearings with Motor Honey. Do not forget this. When the crankshaft is installed you will not be able to easily reach these bearings.

INSTALL THE CRANKSHAFT, MAIN BEARINGS AND MAIN-BEARING SEAL

I always begin any reassembly with the installation of the crankshaft. If the engine is equipped with a rope-style crankshaft seal, you should install it first. Press the rope into the slot in the main housing and carefully cut to shape.

Troubleshooting Gasoline Marine Engines - John Fleming

BE CERTAIN THE SEAL IS SEATED IN THE BOTTOM OF THE GROOVE

Otherwise, the seal will be too short when the pressure is applied; this is very important. Do not let any residue from the cutting or trimming enter the engine block.

Next we will install the top halves of the main bearing shells. Some engine bearings have different shapes or features for the top halves than those for the bottom halves. Be certain that you have all oil holes aligned with any that appear in the block and that the locking tabs on the bearings are in the slots.

Do not oil the main webbings or the backs of the insert halves. They're not supposed to turn in the housing, and they'll get a better grip without the oil. Install the bearing shells by hand, but be careful; they have some fairly sharp surfaces. Once the bearing halves are pressed in place, lubricate them thoroughly. Grease the edge of the rope seal if one is employed.

Check again to be certain that the crankshaft is clean, then generously coat the main journals on the crankshaft with your chosen lubricant. Now carefully, oh so carefully, lower the crankshaft into the bearing halves. Rotate it slowly; it should turn freely.

Obtain a package of Plasti-Gauge. This has a number of plastic strands, each several inches long and with a carefully controlled diameter. From one of those strips cut a series of pieces about one inch long. You will need one for each main bearing. Lay the strips across the journal, one to the bearing.

Lay the main bearing caps out in numerical order on the bench. Wipe the inner surfaces and install the bearing shells into a dry main cap. Be certain the locking tabs are seated in the slots. Liberally coat the outer surfaces of the bearing shells. Install the main caps and torque them down carefully using the exact torque values and sequences described in your service manual. Do not change this procedure in any way.

When the bearings are properly tightened to full torque

Troubleshooting Gasoline Marine Engines - John Fleming

specifications, slowly remove the bolts in reverse order. Carefully remove the main bearing caps. One at a time, remove those plastic strips (which will now be quite flat). Compare the width of the flattened strip to the gauge printed on the paper container that the strips came in. The number that the strip matches on the gauge is the clearance between the bearing and the crankshaft.

The clearance should be .002". A small difference is acceptable, but if the gauge indicates a difference of .001", the crankshaft is not properly fitted. Let me state this another way. If your total clearance is as little as .001", the clearance is not sufficient. If the clearance is as much as .003", the clearance is too great.

If you have done your job properly, an improper clearance at any journal is sufficient to halt operations and consult the machine shop. If the crankshaft is not within tolerance, the machine shop should make any adjustments necessary to correct the problem since they turned the crankshaft.

If a bearing is at fault, the supplier should make any necessary adjustment. Regardless of how you correct this matter, do not assemble the engine if it has a loose or tight bearing. The engine will probably fail. If the problem is extreme, the engine may not turn over at all.

When the bearings show the proper clearance, carefully remove all residue from the Plasti-gauge, lubricate the journals again, and torque the main bearing caps down properly. The crankshaft should be free and turn easily. If it is equipped with a rope seal, it will be a bit tight for a few revolutions, but it should free up quickly.

One of those main bearing shells that you installed had side skirts that overlapped the side of the main-bearing webbing and the main-bearing cap. That is the thrust bearing that accepts the end-thrust loads from the crankshaft.

Using the hammer handle or dowel, tap the crankshaft as far forward as possible, applying only reasonable pressure. Using a feeler gauge, check the clearance between the bearing and the crankshaft. Consult your service manual for the proper figure. If the end clearance is too great, now is the time to find out. This step could not be accomplished during the Plasti-Gauge measurement because the end movement of the crankshaft would have interfered. If every thing checks out, proceed with the assembly.

INSTALL THE PISTONS, RINGS AND INSERT BEARINGS

Take one of the new pistons and turn it upside down in the cylinder bore in which it will eventually run. Carefully push a feeler gauge in between the piston skirt and the cylinder wall. The proper clearance will be given in the service manual for a factory piston, or with the instructions from an aftermarket manufacturer.

Repeat the procedure with each piston.; the clearance for a new piston should be close to minimum. If it is not, consult the machine shop. Do not accept a piston that is out of specification. Next take a piston ring out of the package. Place it in the top of a cylinder bore, and even it up in the cylinder. Check the end gap with a feeler gauge. It must match the specification given on the package or in the service manual. I make this check on three or four cylinders at random, but not necessarily every one unless this is a high-performance engine. If the rings have the proper gap, remove and return them to the proper packages.

I'll assume that the machine shop installed your pistons onto the rods. When you have checked each piston and random piston rings for clearance, remove the connecting-rod cap and its retainer bolts from number #1 piston and set it on the bench.

It is time to install the piston rings. Read the instructions carefully, and replace the rings in the correct order from the top groove to the bottom groove and turn the gaps to the proper position relative to the wrist pin. This is important. Improper placement can cause the engine to use oil or lose

Troubleshooting Gasoline Marine Engines - John Fleming

compression.

When the rings are in their proper places on the piston, place the bearing shells in the top and bottom halves of the connecting rod. As with the main bearing shells, install the bearing onto a dry surface, then liberally coat the bearing surface with lubricant. Be certain that the locking tabs are properly located. Generously lubricate the sides of the pistons and the piston rings with non-detergent cylinder oil. Install a ring compressor onto the piston and tighten it evenly around the rings, first making certain they're still in the proper position.

Remember those short rubber tubes? Install one onto each connecting rod bolt and set the piston assembly into number #1 cylinder. Be certain the numbered side of the connecting-rod faces the outside of the cylinder block. Using a hammer handle or a dowel under the hammer face, lightly tap the piston into the bore. If you should get any solid resistance, stop.

Take the piston out of the bore and adjust the ring compressor. If you have made all of the checks described, the ring compressor is surely your culprit. When it is adjusted properly, the piston will enter the bore, and it can be tapped downward.

Guide the connecting rod onto the rod journal, and be certain that the insert shell is still in the proper position. Remove the rubber tubes and slide the connecting-rod cap onto the retainer bolts. Install the connecting rod bolts and tighten the to 3 lbs./ft. on your torque wrench. Rotate the engine to be certain that it is free.

Install the remaining piston/rod assemblies in the same manner. Rotate the engine as you install each piston/rod assembly. If the engine sticks on any installation, stop and find out why. When all of the piston rod assemblies have been installed properly, turn the engine upside down on the stand and torque all connecting-rod retainer bolts to the factory-recommended specifications.

Turn the engine over as you complete torquing each set

Troubleshooting Gasoline Marine Engines - John Fleming

of connecting-rod bolts. This assures that the engine has not tightened up at any point. Should it do so, you know exactly which assembly offends. When you have properly installed the crankshaft and the piston rod assemblies you have passed a real milestone in engine construction.

Troubleshooting Gasoline Marine Engines - John Fleming

CHAPTER SEVENTEEN
COMPLETE THE ASSEMBLY

The next step is to install the camshaft. This is another critical area, one that is rife with pitfalls. Proceed cautiously.

INSTALL THE CAMSHAFT AND TIMING GEARS

I always lay the engine on its end to install the camshaft. Begin by bolting the camshaft gear lightly onto the camshaft, then liberally coat the journals and the lobes with lubricant. I use Motor Honey on the journals and a heavy black camshaft break-in lubricant on the lobes. (Remember that we lubricated the camshaft bearings at the very start of reassembly.)

Carefully slide the camshaft down into the camshaft bearings. The lobes can destroy the bearings as they pass into the block. This is very important, and much of the success of your work depends upon what you do here. When the camshaft is installed, raise the engine stand to a level position.

Remove the camshaft gear from the camshaft and install the thrust bearing if any is required. Bolt the thrust-bearing retainer into the block, then place the camshaft-drive parts on the bench.

There are two common drive systems. The first is for a normal-rotation engine (left hand on the marine engine). It will ordinarily have two gears, one on the crankshaft and one on

Troubleshooting Gasoline Marine Engines - John Fleming

the camshaft driven by a timing chain. The second is for an opposite-rotation engine (right hand on the marine engine). This system also will generally have two gears, one on the crankshaft and one on the camshaft, but they mesh directly. There will be no chain.

Both assumptions are valid about 95 percent of the time on the engines available today. Assuming the two systems described are employed on any pair of marine engines, the crankshafts will turn in opposite directions, but the camshaft, oil pump and distributor shafts will turn in the same direction. However, you should take nothing for granted. Older or antique engines may have any kind of system. You must have a camshaft and drive system that matches the rotation for the engine you're assembling.

As indicated earlier, you should begin at the first of your tear- down to make absolutely certain that your serial numbers or other indicators of rotational direction are intact. You should also mark any part that you're certain of before removal. I trust that you have done that.

The timing gear set will have a drawing which indicates the proper alignment for the gears and chain and the proper procedure for installation. For an after market part you can use this drawing and these instructions. If you're installing a factory gear and chain set you will use the directions found in the service manual. These will include the proper end play for the camshaft. It is important because excessive end play in the camshaft can ruin the timing gears, the timing chain, the camshaft followers (lifters) and even the camshaft itself.

When the timing gears/chain are properly installed, install a new front seal into the timing-gear cover and fit the new gasket. Install the timing-gear cover on the engine and bolt it in place.

Remember that the front seal is directional, with small striations etched into the lip of the seal, and they're cut at a oblique angle across the sealing surface. If your seal does not match the rotation of the engine, it will pump oil out of the engine. You must be certain that you have bought the proper one. If you're uncertain, look at the angle of attack on the striations. They should be angled into the direction of crankshaft rotation. Apply plenty of Motor Honey, and when the seal is installed, you're ready to turn the engine upside down again.

INSTALL THE OIL PUMP AND PAN

Always install a new oil pump on any rebuild, and never use a high-volume or high-pressure oil pump on a stock engine. The high pressure will "wash" the soft metal out of the bearing shells and possibly lead to early bearing failure. These pumps work well with high-performance engines, but you only need enough pressure to maintain the film on any engine.

The new oil pump will need a new screen and pickup installed. This is another ticklish proposition, and nobody tells you how to do this. I generally use an open-end wrench that fits the flange on the pickup very closely. Align the face of the pickup screen parallel to the machined surface on the mounting flange of the oil pump. Start the pickup assembly into the hole provided for it, and slip the jaws of the wrench over the flange. Use a hammer to tap the wrench handle and drive the pickup tube into the oil pump housing. The flange should go all the way, up flush to the housing.

I often place a small bit of brazing at this junction to prevent the pickup from backing out. If you have properly installed the pickup assembly, it should give no trouble without the brazing.

If you elect to use the same system that I do, be very careful with the brazing process. Too much heat could damage the oil pump or make an air hole in the pickup tube. Attempt this step only if you're experienced with a brazing torch and very confident in your abilities. The brazing process is more important to the high-performance engine than to the stock unit.

There may or may not be a gasket between the oil

Troubleshooting Gasoline Marine Engines - John Fleming

pump and the cylinder block. Your service manual should indicate which is the case with your particular engine. The presence or lack of such a gasket in the gasket set is also an excellent indication.

Never, ever cut a gasket yourself and install it here if one is not indicated by the service manual or provided in the gasket set.

When the oil pump and pickup screen are mounted and the bolts torqued down, you're ready to install the pan. Place the pan gasket over the base of the cylinder block and fit the seal across the bottom of the timing-gear cover. Install the pan and torque the attachment bolts to specification, then turn the engine back upright on the stand.

Install the crankshaft pulley and torque the retainer bolt into place. Using the same wrench, rotate the engine a few times to be sure that it is still free. With the new pistons, piston rings and bearings, the engine will be snug but not bound.

INSTALL THE CAM SHAFT FOLLOWERS

Begin by wiping a bit of lubricant into the lifter bores. I use 30-weight, non-detergent motor oil for this. You can easily use you fingers for this task, but be careful; the block may have a few sharp edges around the lifter bores. I never reuse a set of cam followers (lifters). Take the new lifters from the box.

Liberally coat the bottom of the lifter with the same black camshaft break-in lubricant that you used on the camshaft lobes. Use a squirt can to fill the lifter bodies with lubricant through the side hole. I use the same 30-weight, non-detergent, oil for this as well.

Oil the outside of the lifter body with motor oil and install it into a lifter bore in the block. Camshaft followers for exhaust and intake valves are the same, and there is no special method of installation. Just keep everything clean.

Repeat the process with each of the lifters until all of the bores are full. You have completed the basic engine block and can now proceed to the next phase.

CHAPTER EIGHTEEN
FINAL ENGINE ASSEMBLY

The remainder of the engine assembly is fairly routine. The cylinder heads are the next in order of importance. Be careful how you install the cylinder-head gaskets, and be sure the proper side is up. Never ever use an automotive gasket for this purpose.

Torque the clean and lightly oiled head bolts to factory specifications, following the recommended sequence. When the heads are in place, install the rocker arms. Coat the rocker-arm mounting balls with the black camshaft break-in lubricant and install them onto the rocker studs.

Install the push rods using the same lubricant on the ends of the push rods, and be certain the rocker arms are at least snug enough to hold the push rods in place underneath the rocker arms.

Pour generous amounts of 30-weight non-detergent oil over the rocker arm assemblies, and adjust the rocker arms according to the instructions in the service manual. If you have no manual and if you're using hydraulic lifters, you may use the same procedure for this operation as that described in an automotive manual. Just make certain that the engine for which you're getting instruction has the same block as the one that you're rebuilding. If no service manual of any nature is available, make sure there is a tiny bit of slack between the rocker arm and the valve stem when any given cylinder is on the top of the compression stroke.

Install the new gaskets into the rocker covers and place

Troubleshooting Gasoline Marine Engines - John Fleming

the covers in position atop the cylinder heads. If you were able to adjust the rocker arms properly during installation, bolt the covers into place. If you do not yet have the proper valve adjustment, do not bolt the rocker covers down.

INSTALL THE INTAKE MANIFOLD

Installing an intake manifold often causes problems. You can do this job "wet" (with cement) or "dry" (without cement). The method described in the service manual or by the gasket manufacturer is generally the best. If you feel comfortable with this system, proceed as directed. For my own work, I never use gasket cement on the intake-manifold gaskets on an in-line engine. I sometimes use it for V-6 or V-8 engines.

Intake manifold gaskets for V-6 and V-8s come in four parts. There are two strip gaskets that cover the intake ports themselves and two end seals that cover the ends of the manifold. On certain portions of the manifold gasket set for the V-6 or V-8 engines it may be helpful to use a bit of cement. I suggest you consider the following procedure. Begin with the long strip gaskets that cover the ports. They should be lightly coated with cement, but only in a small spot where the tabs on the end seal overlap, and only on the side towards the cylinder head.

These long strip gaskets can be aligned and supported with a bolt in each end, but they must be held in place and pressed flat against the cylinder head until the cement is dry. When this is complete, remove the bolts. Next, coat the end seals with cement on the side towards the cylinder block only.

Pay particular attention to the small flaps that overlap the manifold gaskets. Do not use large amounts of cement. That will build up a hump, however small, and that hump can effect the seal.

Give the cement on both gasket and seal a reasonable time to dry, then install the intake manifold using the proper bolts with clean and lightly oiled threads. Torque to specification. If you're going to use gasket cement, choose one that is very firm but never gets truly hard.

INSTALL FREEZE PLUGS AND PAINT ENGINE

Using a hammer and a soft wooden dowel, install a new set of brass freeze plugs into the access holes in the cylinder block. I like a dowel that is very nearly the same diameter as the plug; this makes it easier to keep the plug straight.

Now you're ready to paint the engine. Mask off all openings on it and the crankshaft damper. Old spark plugs serve well to close the plug holes in the head. Apply a coat of metal preservative, then two coats of heat-resistant marine-engine paint over the entire surface. Pay careful attention to the crankcase pan, the timing cover and the rocker covers.

These sheet metal parts rust or corrode easily.

The rocker covers or the timing gear cover can usually be replaced with the engine in the boat. Yet, there is always the chance that leakage from a hole in one or the other will destroy an engine. If the crankcase pan develops a hole, it requires removal of the engine to replace a $150 part. These are all rather severe penalties for a small oversight.

THE DIPSTICK TUBE IS IMPORTANT

Paint and replace the dipstick tube. Be careful in installing it so it doesn't leak at the point where it enters the cylinder block. Be certain you have this tube on the proper side. It should be toward the center of the vessel when the engine is installed. On many engine blocks there are openings on both sides, and the tube can be installed on either of them. If this is done improperly, the dipstick could be very hard to reach after the engine is installed.

I usually leave the taping from the paint process in

place over any holes in the block until I'm ready to install a particular accessory. This prevents dust, dirt or other contamination from entering the engine. The engine assembly is complete now and ready for removal from the stand.

THE REAR OF THE ENGINE NEEDS ATTENTION

Remove the engine from the stand and install the crankshaft seal if it was not a rope-style seal and installed previously. The seal housing-to-block gasket should be in your gasket set. Generously coat the sealing surfaces with Motor Honey and torque the housing bolts in place. Install the brass freeze plug into the block over the camshaft rear journal.

Replace all of the screws/plugs that you removed to clean the gallery passages. I use a sealer on the threads. Teflon tape will do, or you can choose any sealer that appeals to you and is recommended for the purpose.

Mask off the seal, then paint the rear end of the engine as you did the cylinder block. Now install the flywheel, drive plate and bell housing in that order. Torque the bolts to factory specifications on clean and lightly oiled threads. If a heat exchanger is provided, it is time to install it, but do not install the hoses. They come later so that wiring may be more easily accomplished.

PRIME THE OILING SYSTEM

At this point I usually prime the oil pump and the moving parts of the engine. Install the oil filter body and spin on a new filter. Put five quarts of oil into the engine. I prefer 30-weight non-detergent motor oil.

Using an old screwdriver whose blade I have cut off at the handle, I insert the blade tip into the drive slot in the oil pump and drive it with a power drill. Continue this until the drill begins to load heavily. When the galleries are full, oil will be pumped into the bearings, pressure will begin to build and the overhead valves and all moving parts of the engine will be lubricated.

Resistance will develop within the system as the oil permeates everything. That pressure will truly load a drill motor and you will have oil pressure before you crank the engine. This concludes the assembly of the engine. Be sure to look for leaks.

Figure 9
John Fleming

This engine is ready for the intake and the accessory installation.

READY FOR THE ACCESSORIES

The first accessory I install is always the distributor. Remove the tape that covered the access hole during painting. Using number #1 cylinder, bring the engine up to top dead

Troubleshooting Gasoline Marine Engines - John Fleming

center on the compression stroke. Both valves should be in the Up (closed) position. The timing mark on the damper should be at 0.

On the distributor cap, locate the position for the #1 cylinder. Make a visible mark on the distributor body in line with this mark, then remove the cap. Turn the rotor to align with that mark. Holding the rotor in the #1 position on the cap, install the distributor.

The distributor drives the oil pump, and if the drive slot in the oil pump shaft is not aligned, you may have a problem trying to install the distributor. That same screwdriver bit that primed the engine can now be used in your hands to align this slot as needed. When you're finished, the engine should be ready to fire the #1 cylinder.

Replace the wiring harness according to the wiring diagram and the number code you applied with those tape strips. Replace the hoses for the heat exchanger using new stainless-steel clamps.

THINGS TO LOOK FOR

Take care to keep the wiring in the proper position, and pay close attention to polarity. Use any wire looms that were in place when you disassembled the engine, and install others at any point where the wiring may hit a hot spot or something likely to chafe.

If you have lost any of the wire-attachment nuts or if any are rusted/corroded, you should replace them with new brass pieces. Do not use ferrous metal, and be certain that you have the proper sizes. Many of these nuts have metric threads.

I always treat a fresh engine to a set of new plug wires as a birthday present. There is simply no reason to ruin or detract from a rather expensive overhaul job otherwise well-done that skips and misses for want of a $50 set of plug leads.

Do not use any kind of gasket sealer between the gaskets on the exhaust manifolds and the exhaust elbows or

Troubleshooting Gasoline Marine Engines - John Fleming

between the exhaust manifolds and the cylinder heads. If these surfaces will not seal, it may be possible to remachine the surfaces, but your best bet is to replace the manifold/elbow. When the sealing surface on any of these parts is less than 3/16" wide (0.1875), I consider it worn out. On rare occasions I have gotten a manifold that was too thin when it was new.

A new exhaust manifold should be at least 1/4" (0.250) in width on all machined sealing surfaces. If your engine has a closed-circuit cooling system with a heat exchanger, the gasket set employed between the exhaust manifold and exhaust elbow will be different from that used on a raw-water cooled engine. Be certain that you have the proper set.

Remember, the rocker covers may not be tight if you were unable to adjust the valves previously. You left the covers loose so they could be adjusted on a running engine. You must still adjust the valves and tighten the covers when you're through.

It is possible on some engines to install the carburetor backwards on the intake manifold. Look at the controls and the choking system for direction. If you're using the old-style, mechanical choke with the spring operated system, always replace the spring assembly on the new engine.

Do not assume the spark plugs that were in the engine were the correct ones. Check the service manual and install a new set with the proper reach and heat range.

Be certain that the proper firing sequence is being observed when you reconnect the leads from the distributor cap to the spark plugs, then make a final check to see if you have forgotten anything.

Everything OK? That priming operation you executed previously also filled the oil filter. Check the dipstick now and add oil to the crankcase if needed.

Put coolant in the heat exchanger if there is one. The thermostat in the engine is closed, and the closed-circuit cooling system is not completely full. When the engine has run for a couple of minutes, check the coolant in the heat exchanger again and refill. It will almost certainly accept a

Troubleshooting Gasoline Marine Engines - John Fleming

significant addition.

You're about ready to crank the engine. I prefer to do so before it is installed in the vessel. This saves a lot of misery over a period of years. Errors are much more easily ministered to in the shop.

If a dynamometer is available, it is desirable to test the engine on this device. If not, it is still wise to run the engine for a short time. During this test you can adjust the valves/rocker arms if they were not done previously.

If you have to adjust the valves during the test run on an old-style (pre-1986) engine, you will probably have to remove the exhaust manifolds after adjustment in order to bolt the rocker covers down. This is unfortunate, but the outside rocker cover bolts often can not be reached with the exhaust manifolds in place.

The engine was left at top dead center on the compression stroke and on #1 cylinder when you installed the distributor. Check to be certain that it is still in that position and proceed as follows:

Remove the spark plug from #1 cylinder. Replace it into the boot on the high-tension wire and lay it on any metal surface of the engine. Back the crankshaft up to 8 degrees before top dead center on the timing mark, and provide current to the ignition system. Slowly rotate the distributor back and forth. The spark plug will fire at some point during this rotation. Watch carefully. If you can stop the rotation just as the plug fires, the distributor is nearly enough in time. Lock it off. You will not get this exactly right the first time or two. However, you have certainly come close enough to start the engine.   There may be another and different procedure suggested by the service manual. If so, you may prefer to use it. The one described above, I discovered quite by accident many years ago, and it certainly works. In any case, always use a timing light before you consider the engine ready to run.

One last check and we will crank this baby! Especially, look for oil or coolant leaks. Remember, you have pressurized the entire oiling system, so you should see any leaks now.

CHAPTER NINETEEN
START-UP PROCEDURE

Any engine going to the dynamometer should be well and adequately handled by the mechanic performing the test. I'll offer a bit of personal advice for those who do not anticipate a dynamometer test.

Attach the engine to water, fuel and battery power. I always prime the fuel system and the carburetor before attempting to crank the engine. This saves unnecessary use of the battery/starter. Be certain the flash arrestor is in place atop the carburetor before attempting to crank the engine.

I use a direct-reading oil-pressure gauge screwed into an oil hole in the gallery. This gives a great deal of assurance during early start-up. You should see pressure on this gauge during the earliest turns of the engine, even on the starter.

Do not grind the starter. Turn the engine over for 15 seconds. If it has not started, back off and let it cool for a moment. Then make another 15-second attempt. If the engine does not crank easily, you have missed something in the assembly or hook-up. Treat the engine exactly as in Chapter One, and look for the reasons why it fails to start.

When the engine starts, the first order of business is to check for oil pressure. Keep the rpm down at this time. This is especially important if the valve lash has not been adjusted.

The second order of business is to adjust the timing. Use a timing light and the specifications from your service manual. The usual numbers are about eight degrees before top dead center, but do not let this replace the proper numbers

Troubleshooting Gasoline Marine Engines - John Fleming

from your manual.

As soon as the engine runs steadily, you may adjust the valves if that is still necessary. There is a procedure for this. You should use the one offered in your service manual, but I'll briefly describe a popular method for certain Chevrolet-based blocks.

Take a wrench that fits the adjustment screw and tighten the tappet until it stops rattling. Then turn the screw 1/2 turn further and you have the proper adjustment. You will have a bit of trouble at first, trying to recognize the point at which the valve actually went silent. This is because there are so many valves making noise.

Run the entire engine, then come back. Loosen the valve adjustment until you can plainly hear it tap This time it should be easy. Repeat the procedure. Tighten the adjustment screw very slowly and listen for the sound to die. Then turn the screw a half-turn farther. When you have repeated this procedure with each valve, they will be well adjusted.

Check again for any coolant or oil leaks, and if none are present, you're ready to install the transmission and move the entire unit to the boat.

As a last effort remove the direct-reading oil gauge and reinstall the plug into the gallery, using Teflon tape or such sealer as you may select. Touch up the paint.

Let us go to the boat.

Troubleshooting Gasoline Marine Engines - John Fleming

CHAPTER TWENTY
PROBLEMS & CAUSE

This chapter will describe the visible ills of the engine and direct your attention in the proper direction for a cure.

We have discussed most or perhaps all of these problems in other chapters, but this is intended as a ready reference. It will allow you to make a rapid run-down for future diagnoses.

THE ENGINE SKIPS OR DOES NOT FIRE

Probable causes are:

No fire in the battery
No fire to the ignition switch
No fire to the ignition coil
Malfunctions in the distributor
Defective plug wires
Defective spark plugs

NO FUEL OR IMPROPER MIXTURE TO THE ENGINE

Probable causes are:

No fuel in the tank
Restrictions in fuel-pick up in tank

Troubleshooting Gasoline Marine Engines - John Fleming

Faulty shut off valve/s
Air or fuel leak in fuel line
Clogged fuel filter
Faulty fuel pump
Carburetor problems

THE ENGINE SMOKES BLACK

The mixture is rich. The carburetor or fuel injector is the probable culprit. If the engine is carbureted, the problem may be:

A stuck float
A failed inlet needle and seat
On some carburetors, a failed power valve
A failed (leaking) diaphragm on the fuel pump
Improper jetting

If the engine is injected the problem may be a clogged injector or an improper signal from the ECM.

THE ENGINE SMOKES GRAY

The engine is burning oil. There are many possible causes, but I'll list a most likely ones:

Failed oil-control rings
Failed valve-guide seals
Too much oil pressure
Too much blow-by

CHECKING THE SPARK-PLUG INSULATORS

Very white colors - Lean mixture
Very dark colors - Rich mixture
Wet insulator - Flooding, thin residue

Wet insulator - Heavy oil consumption heavy residue
Small blisters - Excessive heat
Aluminum beads - Terrific heat, piston is melting.
Broken or cracked porcelain - Can be caused by detonation

OIL LEAKS

Failed gasket
Crankshaft seal has failed.
Crankshaft seal is not proper part.
Excessive back pressure
Leaks in the lube oil heat exchanger

ENGINE OVERHEATS

The possible culprits are:

Intake (raw-water) pickup is clogged
Air leak in intake hose
Raw-water strainer is clogged.
Raw water pump has failed.
Circulating water pump has failed.
The thermostat is stuck.
Cracked cylinder block
Leaking head gasket
Cracked valve seat
Crack(s) in exhaust manifold
Leaking gaskets at manifold/elbow joint
Lack of coolant in the heat exchanger

THE ENGINE USES EXCESSIVE FUEL

Some of the more likely culprits are:
The carburetor or injector is faulty
The timing is too slow (late)

Troubleshooting Gasoline Marine Engines - John Fleming

The spark plugs are worn out
The engine is worn out
The engine is not worn out but has internal problems (i.e. blown head gasket, valves, etc.)
The propeller is too big and the engine is overloaded
The propeller has barnacles/fouling
The boat bottom has barnacles/fouling

THE ENGINE IS HARD TO START

Some possible causes are:

Weak battery
Faulty starter
Faulty carburetor
Poor spark.
Bad spark plugs
Lack of fuel
Spark arrestor is contaminated

THE ENGINE LOSES POWER

Possible causes are:

Restricted fuel flow
Slow timing
Rings are worn out
Blown head gasket
Valves are leaking
Restricted by back pressure (muffler or exhaust line too small, etc.)

THE ENGINE HAS LOW OIL PRESSURE

Some possible causes are:

The lubricant level is low in the engine
The relief valve in the oil pump is stuck
The oil pump is worn out
The engine bearings (rods and/or mains) are worn out
The camshaft bearings are worn out

THE VALVE LIFTERS RATTLE

Possible causes are:

The lubricant level is low
The oil pressure is low
The lifter has failed (stuck)
The rocker arms are out of adjustment
The rocker-arm studs are pulling out of the cylinder head
The push rod has worn, bent or fallen out of the retainer holes
You may be mistaking detonation for vale rattle

THE ENGINE KNOCKS

Some possible causes are:

Excessive valve clearance
Excessive clearance between the wrist pin and the piston
Excessive clearance between the connecting-rod bearing/s and the crankshaft
Excessive clearance between the crankshaft and the main bearing(s)
The timing gears or chain defective

THE ENGINE IS OUT OF TIME

Possible causes are:

Troubleshooting Gasoline Marine Engines - John Fleming

Improper adjustment
Corroded springs in the distributor
Broken or free weights in the distributor
Failed timing gear/chain
The camshaft has broken (not common but it happens)

THE HEAT EXCHANGER LOSES COOLANT

Some possible causes are:

A leak in the tubes
A leaking filler cap
A cracked valve seat
A blown head gasket
A cracked or broken cylinder block

THE BATTERY IS DEAD

Possible causes are:

Low electrolyte in the battery
Dead cell in the battery
A constant drain on the battery with engine shut off (ground, short circuit, etc.)
The alternator does not charge (faulty diode, bad windings, etc.)

THE STARTER MOTOR DOES NOT OPERATE

Some possible causes are:
Faulty battery
Faulty wiring
Faulty starter switch
Faulty solenoid

Troubleshooting Gasoline Marine Engines - John Fleming

Faulty starter motor

THE EXHAUST MANIFOLDS LEAK

Possible causes are:

The manifold-to-elbow gaskets have failed
The manifolds have a crack in the water jackets
The sealing surfaces at the manifold-to-elbow joint have failed

Troubleshooting Gasoline Marine Engines - John Fleming

CHAPTER TWENTY-ONE
TROUBLESHOOT THE ACCESSORIES

The accessories of the engine are very important, and the failure of any has the famous ripple effect where all the parts are in one way or another affected by the failure of a single one. We have touched on the potential problems with the accessories while discussing other phenomena, but thus far we have not explored the individual accessory.

In this chapter we will rectify that. As you read this material, you will realize we're not trying to explain repairs in detail. In many instances it will pay the mechanic to buy a factory-rebuilt part that is easily available, low in price and includes a guarantee.

If the mechanic decides to rebuild the particular accessory himself, then he should consult the service manual for directions. Here we intend to aim you in the right direction.

Some material is redundant. When looking for a specific problem, it is helpful to know the many guises under which it may appear and the several ways to recognize it.

THE DISTRIBUTOR

The parts of the distributor that may fail:

The cap may crack

Troubleshooting Gasoline Marine Engines - John Fleming

The carbon rod in the top of the distributor may fail (break)

The cap may carbon track inside

The rotor may fail (carbon track or ground out to the distributor shaft)

The points may burn, the condenser may fail or the electronic module may fail

The fly weights may freeze or come a loose from their pivots

The springs that tension the flyweights may fail (lose tension, break off or corrode)

The drive gear may fail (strip)

The bearings/bushings on the distributor shaft may wear out

THE CARBURETOR

The parts of the carburetor that may fail are:

The inlet needle and seat
The float (sink or be out of adjustment)
The accelerator pump (bad piston, broken rebound spring)
The jets (clogged, wrong size)
The diaphragm on a four-barrel (does not open secondaries)
The drilled passages (clogged up)
The air-adjustment screws (ringed or ragged needle end)
Leaking gaskets
Worn and leaking throttle shaft
Ruptured power valve

THE ALTERNATOR

The parts of the alternator that may fail are:

Failed ball bearings/bushings
No field excitation
Failed diode/diodes
Failed windings (field coils)
Failed armature
Failed brushes
Failed commutator
Failed connection/s to wiring harness
Drive belt is slipping/missing

THE STARTER

The parts of the starter that may fail are:

The solenoid
The windings
The brushes
The armature
The commutator

THE CIRCULATING WATER PUMP

The parts of the circulating water pump that may fail are:

The drive pulley
The drive belt
The bearings
The input (drive) shaft
The shaft seals
The mounting gaskets
The drive pin that drives the rotor
The rotor itself
Some circulating pumps have aluminum housings, they may corrode

Troubleshooting Gasoline Marine Engines - John Fleming

THE RAW-WATER PUMP

The parts of the raw water pump that may fail are:

The drive pulley
The drive belt
The rubber impeller
The bass or stainless steel cam in the side of the housing
The input shaft
The bearing(s)
The shaft seal

THE OIL PUMP

The parts of the oil pump that may fail are :

The pickup screen may become contaminated (clogged)
The oil-pump drive shaft may fail (be stripped or broken)
The gears in the pump may fail (wear out)

THE OIL FILTER

The parts of the oil-filtration system that may fail are:

The gasket between the filter base and the cylinder block
The gasket between the oil filter body and the base (O-ring)
The filter may fail (clogged)
The pressure relief valve (if so equipped) may fail
The hose connections or the hose on remote mounted filters may fail

Troubleshooting Gasoline Marine Engines - John Fleming

THE RAW-WATER FILTER

The parts of the raw water filter that may fail are:

The gasket
The filter cover (cracks at hose fitting threads)
The filter cover to filter body gasket (O-ring)
The filter body (cracks in plastic body)
The strainer (clogged)

THE ENGINE HEAT EXCHANGER

The parts of the engine heat exchanger that may fail are:

The core coils (leakage, blockage from sedimentation or corrosion)
The end-cap gaskets (between caps and body of heat exchanger)
The zinc anode that protects the unit from corrosion
The pressure cap (loses pressure)

THE LUBE OIL AND TRANSMISSION OIL HEAT EXCHANGERS

The parts of the lube oil and transmission oil heat exchangers that may fail are:

The inner core. (leak oil out of the engine or transmission through the water discharge)
The zinc anode (if so equipped)
As in the other listings of potential problems, you may be able to think of additional possibilities from your own experience. Specific engines may have problems common to that particular power plant that do not appear here. It is not

Troubleshooting Gasoline Marine Engines - John Fleming

possible to denote every problem with every engine, but the foregoing is a comprehensive starting place.

CHAPTER TWENTY-TWO
FINAL WORDS

Think of the principles advanced in these pages as they apply to the theory and operating principles of the engine. In any given situation, think about the things that are not working. Think also about those that are. Of A is working and B is working but C does not work, what parts must operate properly for A and B to perform? Also ask what parts can not possibly work if C has quit?

Eliminate the possible problems in any given situation one logical step at a time. Close your eyes and see the parts. See the circuits and imagine the current flowing down those conductors like water through a pipe. Let your mind see the places where the flow may be interrupted. Consider the kinds of failure that must occur if the flow is to be interrupted. You will often locate the problems that you're faced with by simply thinking about them. So long as the effort represents real concentration, you're still giving good value.

If you want to try for the miracle it is fine by me. In fact, if you want to bring in another mechanic and let him look I'll welcome him to this shop. But if I continue to work on this engine, you will just have to be patient and give me a bit of room because right now I'm stumped.

This is not an easy admission. Pride is wrapped up in our work, and we all like to believe we're the best. But remember this: sooner or later, everybody comes to the lickin' log. The lickin' log was the one that you bent over when you were naughty and Poppa got out the strap. Every mechanic

Troubleshooting Gasoline Marine Engines - John Fleming

will one day bend over that log and take a lickin'

When you find yourself standing in the shadow of that log and fearing the consequence, your head is more likely to get you out of trouble than a great deal of useless activity. So think, damn it!

No amount of thought is wasted, no amount of concentration that will not bear fruit. For many years I looked at exploded views and cut-aways. I ran the engine in my head until every individual part fit into the integrated whole, and all were there on demand.

The crankshaft turned. The camshaft turned at half-speed, the torque twisted the crankshaft and horsepower pulled the load. The plugs fired in sequence, and each cylinder exploded when the fuel/air mix ignited. When you can see the entire operation in your mind, there is no mystery left.

I hope that this work will be of some use to the recreational boater who intends to fix his own engine. I hope it also will be an inspiration to those who intend to be serious mechanics. To each of you I wish the best. It is always a pleasure to work with those who seek to know.

Books published by
Bristol Fashion Publications
Free catalog, phone 1-800-478-7147

Boat Repair Made Easy — Haul Out
Written By John P. Kaufman

Boat Repair Made Easy — Finishes
Written By John P. Kaufman

Boat Repair Made Easy — Systems
Written By John P. Kaufman

Boat Repair Made Easy — Engines
Written By John P. Kaufman

Standard Ship's Log
Designed By John P. Kaufman

Large Ship's Log
Designed By John P. Kaufman

Designing Power & Sail
Written By Arthur Edmunds

Building A Fiberglass Boat
Written By Arthur Edmunds

Buying A Great Boat
Written By Arthur Edmunds

Boater's Book of Nautical Terms
Written By David S. Yetman

Troubleshooting Gasoline Marine Engines - John Fleming

Practical Seamanship
Written By David S. Yetman

Captain Jack's Basic Navigation
Written By Jack I. Davis

Creating Comfort Afloat
Written By Janet Groene

Living Aboard
Written By Janet Groene

Racing The Ice To Cape Horn
Written By Frank Guernsey & Cy Zoerner

Marine Weather Forecasting
Written By J. Frank Brumbaugh

Complete Guide To Gasoline Marine Engines
Written By John Fleming

Complete Guide To Outboard Engines
Written By John Fleming

Complete Guide To Diesel Marine Engines
Written By John Fleming

Trouble Shooting Gasoline Marine Engines
Written By John Fleming

Trailer Boats
Written By Alex Zidock

Skipper's Handbook
Written By Robert S. Grossman

White Squall - The Last Voyage Of Albatross
Written By Richard E. Langford

Troubleshooting Gasoline Marine Engines - John Fleming

**Cruising South
What to Expect Along The ICW**
Written By Joan Healy

Electronics Aboard
Written By Stephen Fishman

**Five Against The Sea
A True Story of Courage & Survival**
Written By Ron Arias

**Scuttlebutt
Seafaring History & Lore**
Written By John Guest

Cruising The South Pacific
Written By Douglas Austin

**Catch of The Day
How To Catch, Clean & Cook It**
Written By Carla Johnson

VHF Marine Radio Handbook
Written By Mike Whitehead

Electric Propulsion For Boats
Written By Charles Mathys

Troubleshooting Gasoline Marine Engines - John Fleming

Troubleshooting Gasoline Marine Engines - John Fleming

ABOUT THE AUTHOR

John Fleming

John Fleming has conducted a 60 year love affair with engines and never met one he did not like. There have been a few that were so exciting he remembers them like an old flame but they all serve a purpose and they are all a part of my memories.

The first engine he built was a 1948 model, 4.2 horsepower, Champion outboard engine. He was 9 years old which made it monumental task. To see and hold the parts his father had described was fascinating.

He held a United States Coast Guard, 500 ton masters ticket and has a total of more than 3,000 days at sea.

John has run boats of many types and varieties in 44 States and 3 countries: crossed the Okefenokee in an airboat and canoe, ran the Everglades from Flamingo Park to Chokloskee Island and from Whitewater Bay to the head of the Little Shark River.

For eight years he held a State of Florida Teachers Certificate to teach engine repair in the State.

John and his wife have run delivery charters across the Gulf of Mexico from Brownsville, Texas to Key West, Florida and up the Atlantic Seaboard as far as Barnegat Bay. They have owned vessels which they have operated for dive charters, fishing charters and towing services.

He has written more than 3,500 articles for magazines and newspapers.

www.ingramcontent.com/pod-product-compliance
Lightning Source LLC
Chambersburg PA
CBHW032259150426
43195CB00008BA/510